9-30-68

THE ECONOMICS OF
TRADING STAMPS

THE ECONOMICS OF
TRADING STAMPS

Harold W. Fox

Public Affairs Press, Washington, D. C.

TO BARBARA

PREFACE

The avalanche of trading stamps during the 1950's was a new experience for many people; for others it evoked memories of long ago. My wife, who remembers helping her grandmother fill saver books, initiated me into the system. It never occurred to us then that ten years later I would embark on an intensive research project that would culminate in this book.

As in the past, controversy continues to surround the stamp system; information on the subject is sparse and even contradictory. Boycotts of supermarkets, according to a leading marketing magazine, presaged the demise of stamps, but a college text published in 1967 states—equally erroneously—that stamp sales are about $9 billion per year. Whereas several large stamp companies claim that their redemption merchandise is worth 2.5% of consumer purchases, a valuation of 1.6% appears in a recent government report. Many other statements about stamps are similarly confusing or do not stand up under investigation.

Hence demands have been mounting for a scrutiny of the economic functions, costs, and benefits of trading stamps. Unfortunately, relatively little is known, for example, about the structure, conduct, and performance of that industry. Who are the leading companies; how do they operate? Under what economic conditions does the stamp system thrive? Why do homemakers and merchants bother with stamps? A thorough appraisal of their significance to consumers, retailers, stamp companies, and the nation's economy is overdue. The purpose of this book is to analyze these and related topics.

Every book is, of course, an intensely personal effort and a characteristically personal product. The strategy of research, the successes and frustrations during the course of investigation, the thrills of discovery and of new insights, and the toil of preparing a study for publication are a writer's individual experience. Yet a book also reflects numerous circumstances and diverse sources. In this case I appreciate above all the American atmosphere of opportunity and the beneficent actions of various teachers and friends. Thanks to the good offices of Professor Harry B. Roggenburg, I interviewed Dr. Eugene R. Beem of The Sperry and Hutchinson Company. It made a grant to the Rutgers University Bureau of Economic Research that defrayed the out-of-pocket cost of the project. Many others—in the industry and outside—generously granted time for interviews and facilitated my research.   Both for their cooperation in providing information and for their respect of my independence, I am truly grateful.

Barbara Fox, my wife, shared with me the pleasures and pains of completing this book.

HAROLD W. FOX

Upsala College
East Orange, New Jersey

CONTENTS

About the Author

Harold W. Fox is a member of the economics faculty of Upsala College, East Orange, New Jersey. He previously taught at the Graduate School of Fairleigh Dickinson University and in the economics department of Rutgers University. His academic credentials include degrees in international marketing, business management, and economics.

A contributor to several books, Dr. Fox also is author of more than a score of articles published in leading scholarly and trade journals. Before entering the academic field, he served as an economic consultant.

CHAPTER I

THE STAMP SYSTEM

Great Britain, which is revered by philatelists as the first nation to issue postage stamps (in 1840) and which was reviled in the previous century for her stamp tax, may be regarded with ambivalence as the land of the first trading stamp. Apparently, a "Blue Trading Stamp Company" operated in England about 1880.[1] The earliest records of trading stamps in the United States date from the 1890's, when Schuster's Department Store of Milwaukee instituted a plan called the Blue Trading Stamp System. In contrast to this user-issuer, The Sperry and Hutchinson Company started in 1896 as an independent issuer. After the turn of the century, stamp plans spread across America and Europe.

Originally, stamps were a cash discount. They were given only on cash sales or on payment within a specified time. In recent years this cash-discount feature has had little importance but in most other basic respects the operation of the system has remained virtually unchanged.

The Trading-Stamp Process. The customary sequence of stamp operations is shown in Figure 1. There are three parties in this process — issuer, user, and saver.

A stamp company — hereinafter called the "issuer" — transfers stamps to a retailer for cash. The stamp company retains title, thus reserving certain legal rights. (In this book such expressions as selling or buying of stamps always mean transfers subject to any rights reserved by the issuer.) Along with the stamps the company gives the retailer free catalogs, saver books, advertising, and advice.

The contracting retailer — called the "user" here — disburses the trading stamps to his customers. The basic rate is 1 per ten-cent sale but, on occasion, users give extra stamps. The retailer also passes on the catalogs and saver books.

The customer — a "saver" — pastes stamps into booklets and accumulates them for the premiums listed in the catalog. The unit of account in the latter is not dollars but filled saver books. When the saver has filled the requisite number of books, he goes to a redemption center operated by the trading-stamp company and claims the desired merchandise. The consumer's interest is sustained or heightened by

1

Figure 1

STRUCTURE OF THE TRADING STAMP PROCESS

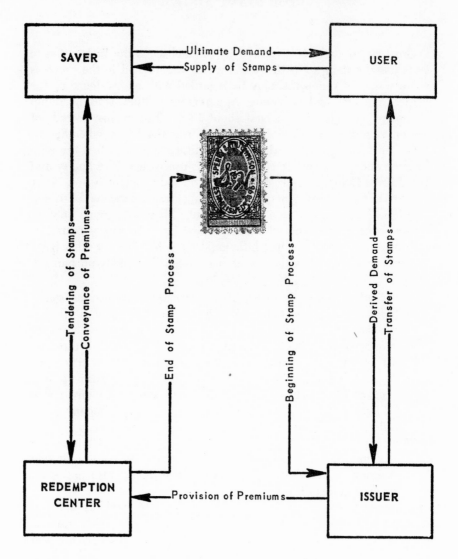

satisfaction with the system plus reminder advertising by the issuer and the user.

Over the years the industry has flourished and foundered and forged ahead again. Until World War I the system enjoyed a surge of popularity; another, stronger tide of enthusiasm swept the United States after 1951. The last-mentioned boom — which currently shows signs of abating — is the reference period for the research discussed in this study of the stamps' economic functions, costs, and benefits. The system has economic significance to consumers, retailers, stamp companies, and others in the economy; an examination of these influences seems to be overdue.

Economic Research on Trading Stamps. In spite of lively interest in trading stamps, very few economists have dealt with them. Among the works published thus far, two are especially illuminating: Vredenburg's study at the beginning of the current American stamp boom and Fulop's analysis in Great Britain.[2]

Economic research on the subject has been frequently urged. For example, in 1962 a legally oriented study concluded after 138 pages and 211 footnotes that "Further examination of the trading-stamp industry and its effects on the economy would appear useful . . ."[3] Two years later the Legislative Research Council of the Commonwealth of Massachusetts in its 101-page document could still note: "No major report on the economics of trading stamps has appeared since stamps began saturating the food marketing business."[4]

A letter to the author, dated September 23, 1965, from the Executive Office of the President of the United States singled out the Agriculture Department study of 1958[5] as the most comprehensive government research on the subject. "But," continued Mrs. Esther Peterson, then Special Assistant to the President for Consumer Affairs, "I believe further study is needed in the light of the marketing changes that have taken place in the last seven years."

A topic of particular interest to consumers and policy makers is the economic aspect of the industry's distribution of redemption merchandise. "Whether this system of marketing these items is more efficient than the more conventional methods is an important question . . ." stated the Agricultural Marketing Service in a research report.[6] In the 80th Congress, Representative Lester L. Wolff offered an amendment to the "Truth in Packaging" Bill which would have required the issuers to set forth on the face of each stamp its "true value" and to state in any catalogs or advertising the monetary value of the premiums offered.[7] Every year, other law-making or law-enforcing bodies also consider various ramifications of trading stamps.

Outline of the Book. To refer again to Figure 1, this work starts at the center and then proceeds clockwise from the top left corner. Thus, topics will appear in the following order: stamp — saver — user — issuer — premium.

The stamp is the organizing nexus for a far flung consumer-marketing operation. After a comparison, in Chapter II, of its functions to those of money, the focus shifts to the participants in the process.

The terms "demand" and "supply" are employed to denote the schedules of stamp quantities sought and disbursed with their corresponding (financial or nonfinancial) values to consumers and retailers, respectively. In 1967, more than eight out of every ten households, in every state of the Union, saved trading stamps. Chapter III probes this demand. The supply side, encompassing some 250,000 retailers which account for about one-seventh of all retail volume, is discussed in Chapters IV and V.

These saver and retail activities are coordinated by a service industry: the issuers. Chapter VI and VII analyze the industry's structure and its environment. The operations and financial data of the issuers are scrutinized in Chapter VIII. Next, the value of redemption merchandise, a subject long in dispute, is discussed in Chapter IX. Chapter X contains the findings of a pricing study conducted by the writer for the purpose of estimating the value of premiums. These research results permit an evaluation of the benefit that S & H (Sperry and Hutchinson) stamps provide to savers in relation to the average price paid by retailers for the stamps.

Among economists there is a perennial suspicion that retail prices are unnecessarily high, the excess arising from the existence of more stores than essential to satisfy consumers. A century ago when stamps did not exist, other forms of promotion were less common, and there were few large retailers, the actual retail structure may have conformed more closely than now to the model of perfect competition. But even in that climate a leading economics text stated: "Retail price, the price paid by the actual consumer, seems to feel very slowly and imperfectly the effect of competition; and when competition does exist, it often, instead of lowering prices, merely divides the gains of the price among a greater number of dealers."[8]

Whether trading stamps aggravate the tendency toward high prices has not been resolved but Chapter XI presents some theoretical and empirical analyses of this question. Since the retail sector of the American economy is open to innovators and experimenters, actual cost incidence depends heavily on consumers' day-by-day responsiveness to price cuts as compared to other promotions. When the percentage increase in sales exceeds the percentage decrease in price, demand is elastic and price cuts may be more effective than other methods. Finally, to help the reader form his own judgment about the stamp system, Chapter XII summarizes some of the key findings of this study.

Since the emphasis is economic, contributions from other sciences are generally excluded. There are some findings in anthropology, however, that should be mentioned. In searching for explanations of the system's appeal the concept of a gift to the customer intruded recurrently. The gift as an element in a mercantile transaction has a pre-economic root of which the trading stamp appears to be a modern version.

In virtually all primitive societies studied, anthropologists have found that division of labor was assigned through certain ceremonies. "The form usually taken is that of the gift generously offered; but the accompanying behaviour is formal pretence and social deception, while the transaction itself is based on obligation and economic self-interest." [9] "Among things exchanged are tokens of wealth, a kind of money." [10] Far from altruism, the early significance of a gift is the creation of an obligation from the recipient to the donor. The present tied the receiver to the giver. Early systems of gifts also had religious connotations which are not relevant to this study. But "these gifts . . . are for the most part . . . to maintain a profitable alliance." [11]

Some of the social aspects of this gift-giving heritage survive in such everyday compulsions as to accept invitations and to return them, to exchange Christmas cards, or to show gratitude for favors bestowed. The socio-economic factors could be examined in great detail — they are worthy studies in themselves — but the direction here is economic. The fact remains, however, that what currently appears to be simply a merchandising tool which may or may not be effective and worthwhile, is woven into the fabric of social as well as economic patterns and on occasion may defy analysis in solely economic terms.

Chapter II

QUASI-CURRENCY

The ubiquitousness of trading stamps evokes many attempts at explanation in terms of different frames of reference. Reactions to stamps vary but are rarely neutral. Some people disdain them as if they were the root of all evil. But on many others they exert a real fascination. Perhaps they are regarded like savings in a piggy bank, available to be spent — surely an attractive attribute. This savability-spendability feature may indeed be a cause of the widespread interest.

Resemblances to Money. In a first attempt to trace the economic role of trading stamps one is struck by their physical and functional resemblance to money. The physical similarity is plainly evident. Not only are the miniatures frequently green or gold, they also are issued in various denominations. The divisible unit of account has many advantages. It lowers the issuer's cost of printing. It reduces the user's task in handling. And it eases the saver's pasting chore. All of these benefits of multiple denominations are similar to multi-units of currency and facilitate its emission, disbursement, and storage.

At a slightly less superficial level, trading stamps can be seen to take on several money-like roles at various stages of their service. While the saver is accumulating his treasure they are a store of value. Since they are desired for the redemption merchandise they can command, their acceptability depends on a sound premium standard. The catalogs offer a limited selection of goods which are priced in units of full and fractional saver books. For these premiums the trading stamp serves as a unit of account. When, on special orders, the issuer supplies the needs of eleemosynary organizations or community groups, this accounting unit is extended even further. It is the basis for reckoning not only the transaction between the group and the stamp company, but also for the accounting between the group and its member-supporters during the drive to assemble the necessary purchasing power.

During the course of the stamp process the gummed papers are "a temporary abode of purchasing power enabling the act of purchase to be separated from the act of sale," which is the concept that Friedman and Schwartz mentioned in their analysis of money.[1] The saver is holding a claim that he can settle in the future at a redemption center. Thus they also serve as a standard for deferred transactions. Tendered for a premium, they are a medium of exchange. Carefully supervised destruction ends the process.

Differences From Money. If these diverse roles assumed by the trading stamp are examined more closely it is seen that they are not all of equal importance. It is more a store of value than a medium of exchange. Irregular receipt, pasting, etc. may be inconvenient but saver booklets are as easy to store as currency. They are kept an average of six to nine months before they are spent for merchandise. This implies a velocity of 1.6. In contrast, the transaction velocity of money is over 8½ times higher. Stamps cannot be deposited in a savings account but the amount of interest that could be earned on a comparable accumulation of money is less than a dime.

As a temporary store of value and a standard of deferred transactions the trading stamp may, at times, be superior to money. Although policies vary among companies, over the life of a premium catalog (say, a year) the number of books required to redeem listed merchandise ordinarily does not increase. As a going concern the firm covers its predicted requirements systematically and does not make minor adjustments in its denominator. Thus it insulates the saver from fluctuations in the unit of account. In contrast, within nearly every year after 1940 the value of money has declined. During 1966, for example, the purchasing power of the dollar decreased about 3%. Thus, if issuers do not pass forward the price increases, the trading stamp to that extent is a better medium than money for saving toward an article during a modest inflation. The converse would obtain during deflation. The fact that, historically, stamps have been popular during periods of gently rising prices and weak during both price declines and sharp inflations may be a coincidence, but it also is consistent with maximization of consumer purchasing power.

Although stamps perform satisfactorily as a temporary store of value, they have critical limitations as medium of exchange. Their purchasing power is restricted and their circulation impractical. Transferability after disbursement by retailers is of concern to both the consumer and the issuer. Indeed, brokerage houses operate from time to time, reallocating outstanding stamps. On the part of consumers interest in exchange arises from persons wishing to dispose of stamps and persons who seek to acquire them. There are three main consumer sources: persons who shift from one store to another and have some accumulation of the former brand available for exchange; customers who receive stamps but choose not to save them; and savers who feel they can do better by shopping with cash — or who do not have enough books as yet for an item — and hence liquidate their stamps to use the cash for purchasing the wanted article.

In contrast, some savers might wish to obtain additional stamps for other brands or for cash. Some people have their sights on an article that, at the redemption rate, can be acquired more cheaply with stamps than with cash. Certain items may be available more readily at a redemption center than at a retail store, so for other persons it may be more convenient to procure stamps than to search for the desired goods. Of greater importance is the demand from savers who want a listed article before they have accumulated enough books. As the consumer approaches his goal, the lacking stamps become increasingly more desirable. Hence some savers would be willing to pay a premium at a bourse.

Since such formal exchanges are only occasionally active and since the redemption rate of established trading-stamp companies reportedly is very high, apparently "odd lots" are disposed of through normal channels without the services of extra intermediaries. These interchanges are unfair practices as far as the issuers are concerned. The basic objection to arbitraging is that it destroys the continuity-of-saving feature which is vital to a stamp plan's operation. Payment of handling fees or outright sale of stamps destroys the gift image. The possibility of "price cutting" threatens the equilibrium of low cross-elasticity of demand. Another important objection to commercial stamp brokers is that a cash-purchase offer provides a substitute for the redemption center's monopoly and invites an opportunity to exploit the uninformed.

In addition to opposing exchange-for-fee markets the stamp companies have also waged legal actions against merchants who without authorization disburse, exchange, or redeem stamps. Perhaps the most important outlet for "black-market" stamps is retailers who cannot get a particular brand directly because of franchising restrictions. As far back as 1904 and 1905, courts in Rhode Island, Massachusetts, and Pennsylvania enjoined such bootlegging. There have been quite a few cases on illegal trafficking in stamps since then. Several years ago, an offender was jailed for contempt of a New York court and for refusal to pay a fine.

The stamp companies do not want unlicensed dealers to infringe on the relationships among the issuers, the users, and the stamp-saving customers. Unauthorized stamp usage usurps the issuer's goodwill, an

Oklahoma court held in 1965.[2] Courts also have found that the transferability restriction on theater tickets and premium coupons is a precedent for stamps. In practice, diversion of stamps is negligible — it affects a tiny fraction of a per cent of all those outstanding, but diversion might be more frequent if the issuers did not oppose it.

The companies code their issues — just as the Mint does — for various internal purposes. But after the stamps leave the retailer, it is very difficult to prevent negotiation of the bearer instruments. As a matter of goodwill and expediency, issuers usually allow individual savers to exchange stamps privately. Many companies actually encourage savers to donate them for charitable purposes. In some instances large companies have honored the emissions of defunct firms as an investment to promote public trust and to forestall adverse legislation. But on the whole, issuers have opposed general convertibility while opponents of stamps advocate it. The latter argue that rescission of the stamp company's property right would promote the savers' freedom of choice and even increase acceptance of the system.

Since stamps do not have horizontal convertibility (one brand for another) at present, this idea has great appeal to some consumers. If horizontal convertibility were required by law, how it would work out and how much additional effort people would be willing to exert to take advantage of it, would have to be demonstrated. Clearly, however, the costs of administering such an operation would tend to lower redemption values, perhaps quite substantially.

Vertical convertibility (cash redemption) has been of little interest to consumers although the option is required, as of April 1967, in sixteen states. In addition to the "option" states, three effectively allow cash redemption only. In that event redeemable quantities of stamps become the equivalent of commercial paper (bearer notes redeemable on demand). As might be expected, the stamp company cannot pay more to the saver than the factory cost of merchandise plus any out-of-pocket expense savings. Hence the cash value is likely to be less than the retail values of the premiums, and the cash option is seldom exercised. Even where the two values are close, a very high proportion of savers has manifested liquidity abstinence. This election appears to permeate consumer attitudes toward stamps. Hence it will be a recurring theme in the next chapter.

The limited transferability of trading stamps sets them apart from money, despite the many money-like functions that they perform. This convertibility restriction is crucial. Horizontal exchange, i.e., stamps-for-other-brands, greatly impairs the system's effectiveness for the retailer; vertical exchange, i.e., stamps-for-cash, lessens its function for the consumer.

Stamps Are Not Money. The indeterminate nature of stamps, with their close resemblance to but critical difference from small amounts of money, has elicited conflicting appraisals from consumer advisory groups. Consumers Union excludes the quasi-currency from the money budget and advises its members to shop on the basis of price and quality. Stamps should be accepted only as something extra.[3] In contrast, the Consumer Interests Committee of the American Home Economics Association feels that "cash spending and stamp book 'spending' (redemption of filled books) is more effective if coordinated in an overall plan." Accordingly Professor L. D. Morse, the committee's chairman, objects to the "multiple currency market" caused by stamps.[4] Citing their connection with the efficiency of the market, simplification of terms of trade, and reduction of confusion among buyers and sellers, Professor Morse questions the impact of stamps on the "ever increasing cost to the consumer, that is, the cost of marketing." His committee's resolutions to proscribe and to condemn trading stamps were not adopted by the Association.

Regardless of shopping strategy, it is clear that trading stamps are not money; in fact, printing of money under private auspices is illegal. Neither are they securities. Stamps are primarily a promotional service which, in practice, takes the form of a noninterest-bearing fractional merchandise certificate toward a limited range of spending. Available only with the purchase of merchandise or under special conditions, they lack government backing. The issuer can change their value at will. Some of these differences from money seem to be obvious limitations yet they can be the very source of the stamp's usefulness to consumers and retailers.

Money Inflation Versus Stamp Inflation. In a period of general inflation, a flight from money ensues. If stamp issuers raised their quotations for premiums, stamps, too, would depreciate in value but— as will be shown below—inflation in their use may invite a flight to them.

First, a theoretical demonstration of why stamps are not functional when all resources are fully employed and fixed, as presented by Davis.[5] If the money supply and velocity remain unchanged, all factors of production are competitively priced, and all retailers' input-output relations equally amenable to stamps, a universal adoption would solely lead to a rise in the price level. Some of the goods whose total supply is fixed would be diverted to redemption centers; retailers would charge the same total amount as before stamp adoption, but for a lesser quantity of goods available for sale. The consumer, however, would still get the same total amount of merchandise as before: in part from the retailers and the balance from redemption centers. Thus stamps would have caused a rise in the monetary price level but the real price level would be the same as it had been before their introduction.

There is a practical counterpart to Davis' theoretical analysis. Since the value of premiums that the saver obtains is excluded from the Consumer Price Index, this standard indicator would record only a rise in prices, a nominal rise due to stamps, and ignore the compensating benefit. What about inflation in the medium itself?

A large increase in the supply of trading stamps has a different effect. As they become more abundant, both consumers' fervor and retailers' distaste for stamps increase. Here is an example. Although most issuers protect their accounts or at least key accounts through franchises, in California a group of businessmen instituted an unrestricted stamp plan and its brand was disbursed by numerous competing retailers. Instead of wearying of the omnipresent adhesives, people saved them with greater enthusiasm. "Apparently, as stamps become more easily available more people not only adopt the saving habit, but those who have already started saving increase the amount of their saving," concluded Forbes Research, Inc.[6] Thus excess does not end this fashion.

It should be pointed out, however, that the consumers' stamp-profusion preference is liable to be as illusory as a clamor for "easy money." A superabundance of money causes a price rise. Although "easy stamps" could, by making gifts available on a larger portion of consumer purchases, make it simpler to qualify for premiums, the main effect would be to put cost pressure on the participating retailers. If all competing stores disburse the same brand of stamp, the vehicle confers no distinctiveness and, therefore, can be only defensive. Not surprisingly, the Super Market Institute found that in 1962 nearly three of four members in the Pacific region felt that stamps were not producing sufficient sales gains to absorb the cost—which was the reverse of the tally in the rest of the country.[7] Apparently, undue proliferation need not, but is likely to, lead to price increases or a lessening in stamp use. The similarity to monetary policy holds also for the converse situation. A condition of "tight stamps" chokes off the boom;

it takes too long to qualify for premiums. Thus money inflation and stamp inflation are somewhat analogous.

Stamps operate—on a very small scale—like an "elastic currency." With disbursement at a fixed rate, a user's promotional support expands when business is brisk and contracts when volume slackens. This is inappropriate in those situations where the emphasis should be contra-cyclical. When consumers' receipts of the gift dwindle (as in a depression) and when people worry about basic needs, the functions of money provide greater utility than those of stamps.

Summary. Although trading stamps perform some functions as if they were currency, the ways in which they are used or not used lead to the conclusion that they are not money. Yet for many savers they are a welcome supplement to the family budget. The diversity of views—among and within consumer groups—testifies to the difficulty of categorizing this hybrid instrument. Like consumer groups, economists also differ in their interpretation. Since the stamp combines all elements of the marketing mix it is often considered a selling cost but it fits the criteria of a production cost in Professor Chamberlin's classification schema.

Finally, the absolute-value difference should not be overlooked. Relative to the sales of the merchant or the purchases of the consumer, stamps never amount to more than a very small portion of total expenditures. The basic unit of account is, after all, only a fraction of a penny. Perhaps the fact that it is not petty cash is what helps make the quasi-currency popular.

CHAPTER III

CONSUMER DEMAND

"The enchantment of the consumer with trading stamps often defies reason or logic," observes a report by the Massachusetts Legislative Research Council. This mystery is worth exploring; the consumer's reaction to stamps is the key to the system's existence. Prior to World War I, the quasi-currency enjoyed a surge of popularity—to be followed by more than three decades of public apathy.

Nobody understands all the subtleties of human behavior. Historically, during depressions interest in stamps has waned. It may be they were not properly used; perhaps people regarded them as frivolous. But it seems plausible that under more propitious circumstances, a depression-raised generation will be disposed toward saving, even if the potential seems small. In the early 1950's, homemakers clamored for stamps as grocery stores and gasoline stations became the two main conduits. The operation of the system in these two types of retail establishments during the contemporary stamp success is the frame of reference for the consumer analysis which follows.

The Consumer as Shopper. An analysis of consumers' behavior in a free economy must take account of consumer heterogeneity. The market place must accommodate many diverse tastes. For example, in the 1950's the explosive demand for trading stamps and other extra services in supermarkets coincided with the rise of general-merchandise discount houses which operated in an atmosphere of austerity. In the mid-1960's discount operations spread to food but, at the same time, frankly high-cost "convenience stores" enjoyed increasing patronage. In markets distinguished by such multiformity, it is not surprising that trading stamps could be effective, popular, and widely used in some lines at the same time that they were ineffective and hardly used at all elsewhere.

The modern shopper for staples faces a frequent, repetitious, and time-consuming task. The most likely purchasing agent is the wife, even though one-third of all women are in the labor force and even though the task is sometimes carried out by a man or family group. In the time that she can allot from household chores, economic work, and social activities, the shopper evaluates food stores on the basis of location, assortment and quality of goods, prices, atmosphere, and shopping convenience. The housewife also notes advertisements and listens to recommendations from neighbors. Before the 1950's very few supermarkets gave trading stamps; it is only since then that they have become a factor in her consideration.

She finds that it is extremely time-consuming to shop several stores—comparing just three may entail five visits to get the best price on every item. The combinations and permutations become confusing, so that the effort may lack a pay-off. Parking, comparing, waiting at the checkout take a great deal of time and energy. To conserve her strength, she may rotate among eligible stores, yet often after a number of trips no one store emerges that gives a consistent price advantage. Each store seems to be competitive, possibly a result of deliberate pricing tactics. In passing it should be mentioned that in the modern American market, opportunities due to economic growth, family mobility, and consumer receptivity to service beckon into retailing many ingenious or daring entrants who are undeterred by the high incidence of failure. Thus the institutional setting, consumer behavior, and the supply function negate the tendency toward a capacity-demand equilibrium that obtains in the economic model of perfect competition. Curiosity or convenience will attract some consumers to newly opened stores—until many stores exist, often with considerable idle capacity. If all local supermarkets seem to score about equally, the consumer has little preference and shopping is done more or less by chance among several establishments. "Normal human nature does not bother about very small things. Even the most careful housewife, with a large family and a very small income, has to draw the line somewhere," [1] explains a leading text on economic theory.

Apparently, some consumer demand curves have a zone of price indifference or nondiscernment around the market-price level. The size of this inelastic segment depends on the consumer's valuation of her time and effort. Nevertheless, grocers cannot exploit this zone of price nondiscernment by raising prices within it because everybody's focus of attention is different. Some shoppers will be far more price sensitive than others. On frequently bought items, the family purchasing agent may have a good idea of the approximate market price, based on her experience and her attention to a continuing influx of information. A few items which are consumed in most households may be used as indicators of a store's price level and carefully watched in many households. Due to the diversity of consumption habits, alertness to other items is scattered. But even on specialties the merchant's penalty is high for a noticeable departure from the prevailing price. For example, dietetic food may account for only one-third of 1% of a supermarket's volume, but in any such category, perhaps 80% of the purchases are made by 20% of the shoppers. Among these 20%, many will be "experts" on "their" category—the retailer who would hide a price increase among an insignificant one-third of 1% of sales gambles with alienating 20% of his customers. Thus the "nondiscernment" grants the merchant little opportunity for exploitation. The same is true in the opposite direction since competitors cannot ignore a noticeable price cut, unless there are major differences in other aspects of operation. Generally, the price offerings of merchants are likely to be similar.

Thus with prices and services tending to be alike, the consumer continues to award her patronage impartially as long as a systematic attachment goes unrewarded. It is in such a situation that an introduction of trading stamps can be very effective for the retailer, provided the consumer responds to the system.

Due to this deferred discount, a shopper may cease to be neutral about her supplier. To optimize the receipt of stamps, the family purchasing agent may change to a particular store, shop at a particular time, give preference to featured goods . . . The gift motivates these shopping adjustments. It rewards an effort for which no cash wages are collected.

Consumer Choice. After stamps are introduced, the consumer has several choices. She can shop in stores that do not give stamps or that offer other attractions. She can shift to stamp-givers provided their prices are in line with the nonstamp stores or even if their prices do reflect the extra cost.

If the consumer votes against stamps, the trend toward numerous stores—high-cost producers operating far below capacity—is likely to continue. This is primarily due to ease of entry into retailing, as explained in Chapter IV.

If she transfers her patronage from nonusers to users, the latter will gain largely at the expense of the former because, at one point in time, the total consumption of food and gasoline is almost fixed. When the saver buys groceries and also gets stamps at the same price as she would have paid for the groceries alone, she reaps a surplus. If the retailer continues in business even though the extra expense cuts into his profit, the implication is that trading stamps represent a transfer to consumer surplus from economic rent. If the patron is satisfied with retailing services even after some nondisbursers have withdrawn from the market, there is an implication that the retired factors had been an inefficient allocation of resources. The limited amount of monopoly power obtained by franchised stores is checked on the demand side by consumer diversity, mobility, and mutability. It is checked on the supply side by innovation.

Finally, if the family purchasing agent prefers to divide her business among numerous stores and insists on stamps, she must pay for them in the form of higher prices. The choice is up to the consumer.

Sometimes the choice has been made known with dramatic effect. When the Tennessee Legislature enacted a law against trading stamps in 1957, it was flooded with over forty thousand letters of protest and a group of housewives picketed the Capitol. In a 1959 Supreme Court decision Justice Felix Frankfurter referred to an antistamp bill in Colorado that brought a batallion of irate housewives to the legislature. One of the Colorado sponsors withdrew when his mother threatened to campaign against him the next time he stood for election.[2] In fact, trading stamps once had the distinction of outpolling President Eisenhower at the height of his popularity. In the election of 1956, the normally Republican state of North Dakota put a new prohibition of them to a referendum. The citizens swept the Republican candidate into the governor's chair with 147,400 votes; President Eisenhower won the state with a landslide of 156,766; while 159,801 citizens voted in favor of trading stamps.

Although the majority of United States adults endorses trading stamps (see Table 2), the minority that favors stamp abstinence can for the most part exercise its choice. A possible exception is California where penetration is deep but occurs under circumstances in which the state's leading issuer may have violated the Sherman Antitrust Act.

The prevalent situation is reflected in the fact that, even at the crest of their popularity, stamps accompanied less than 50% of all grocery-store sales. In all other types of retailing, the volume tied to stamps has always been much smaller. The grocery trade includes many stores that "have continued to give very heavy emphasis to price" or tried to develop a "food discounting" image, as the National Commission on Food Marketing noted: "While this 'price competition' alternative is offered to consumers on a significant scale, it is not at all clear that consumers want straight-price competition. While there are some subgroups whose price sensitivity remains high, it appears that the main stream of consumers is increasingly sensitive to . . . trading stamps, et cetera."[3]

In sum, the consumer appears to be highly motivated toward stamps and to resist attempts to prohibit their use. Offered a choice between them and other benefits, there is considerable evidence that throughout the 1950's and 1960's the patrons of grocery stores and gas stations often elected stamps.

Consumer Wants and Satisfactions. Why has the stamp system evoked such widespread support? Shoppers who find the stamp attractive respond to it for many reasons. It helps to fill wants already existing in the consumer's own background and attitude. The American adult of the 1950's typically found himself (or herself) with a growing family, a growing perspective for material possessions, a growing sensation of busyness, and a growing amount of debt. The long depression, World War II, reconversion delays, and the Korean conflict had created a tremendous backlog of household needs. A rising trend in income (ability to buy) and confidence (willingness to buy) nourished a long expansion in demand. Although far from universal, this burgeoning demand was quite broadly based.

Since the end of World War II, George Katona has regularly probed the economic aspects of changes in consumers' attitudes. He noted that ownership of wealth inspires a further achievement orientation. Accomplishment and ownership raise the horizon of wants. Achievers are future-oriented and optimistic. These findings are consistent with the great popularity of trading stamps. The following of stamps is especially prominent among families who are striving to attain or surpass the average of national income. The gap between what these self-styled middle-class households want and what they own is, to a large extent, the type of personal belongings that is available through premiums. "Stamps apparently raise the quality standards," according to merchandising expert Bernice Fitz-Gibbon. ". . . The average woman saves stamps in order to obtain nicer things than she would normally purchase."[4] Professors Wallace O. Yoder and Ronald R. Larson discovered that far from breaking the habit, a redemption of saver books reinforces it. One accomplishment leads to another.[5]

It seems many families adjust their scale of living to an expected income in an upward extrapolated range. Consumer indebtedness has soared; fixed commitments have usurped a rising share of the growing current income. Along with the increasing financial commitment exists the social commitment to what Nassau Senior, a 19th century economist, has called the "decencies." They are the goods that an individual needs to preserve his rank in society. And a leading modern theorist of consumer behavior has explained that "ours is a society in which one of the principal social goals is the higher standard of living. . . . The desire to get superior goods takes on a life of its own."[6] In the United States, another economist pointed out, consumer goods confer on their owner the type of prestige that in many foreign countries is reserved for the man of aristocratic breeding or intellectual superiority. Further, the American drive for consumption is propelled by the attainability and attractiveness of the goods; it is directed "by the unusual power of women."[7]

The relevance to redemption merchandise is manifest. The homemaker wants the premiums, for the reasons cited, and many catalog listings are within easy reach. For example, in 1955 The Sperry and Hutchinson Company listed 106 items requiring one book; in 1960, 189; and in 1965, 249. Some other firms, among them The Triple-S Stamp Company, feature dozens of premiums for as little as one-quarter or one-half book. Thus a saver can easily qualify for many wanted goods. A family spending about $1,500 per year in stamp-giving stores can fill one book every month—extra stamps enable the saver to complete a book even faster.

Although most stamp plans provide for a standard disbursement ratio of 1 per ten-cent sale, there are at least four forms of exceeding this norm: institutional, multiple, prize, and bonus quantities. The first supplement is on a minimum amount of total purchases, often awarded on special days only; the second is a higher norm such as double or triple stamping on all goods; the third is an award to winners, as in a contest or drawing; the fourth is a surplus inducement on a particular item. On the other hand, the user's ratio may be less than standard since there are some goods which by law or custom are exempt from stamps, and there is breakage: the customer does not get one on the expenditure portion under a full ten cents (on $1.49 the usual quantity is 14 stamps).

According to consumer surveys, serious interest in stamps has been quite broadly based. The following tables summarize the findings on the popularity of trading stamps in the United States and the demographic background of savers.

In a population with as many unlike tastes as characterize American families, the persistent participation level in the 80% range achieved by trading stamps is a rare showing of near-unanimity. Some dissent would, of course, be expected. But in eight recent years, people who

Table 1

ATTITUDES TOWARD TRADING STAMPS AND ANALYSIS OF SAVERS
PERCENTAGES OF UNITED STATES HOUSEHOLDS, 1959 TO 1966

United States Households	1959	1960	1961	1962	1963	1964	1965	1966
Total (000)	51,217	52,515	53,800	54,600	55,500	56,300	57,200	58,092
PERCENTAGES								
Say They Like Stamps	76	75	72	72	72	72	76	74
Want State Gov't to Discontinue Stamps	7	6	6	6	7	7	6	5
Save Stamps for Redemption	77	77	76	84	81	85	84	85
OCCUPATION								
Professional and Managerial	73	81	75	82	82	84	87	87
Clerical and Sales	80	73	78	84	87	90	85	83
Skilled and Semi-Skilled	80	82	83	88	86	87	85	88
Service and Labor	76	78	74	89	80	89	88	87
Farm and Farm Labor	70	71	68	78	72	75	76	78
FAMILY INCOME								
Under $3,000	71	66	60	75	67	76	74	74
$3,000 to $4,999	79	78	79	85	82	86	81	85
$5,000 to $6,999	81	80	82	88	86	87	86	88
$7,000 and Over	74	80	78	86	84	87	87	87
FAMILY SIZE								
One or Two	68	69	66	77	75	80	77	81
Three or Four	81	80	82	86	84	87	86	87
Five or More	83	84	80	90	85	88	88	88
CITY AREA								
Over 1,000,000	73	74	79	85	81	86	83	} 86
50,000 to 1,000,000	75	75	73	88	82	85	85	} 86
2,500 to 49,999	85	83	71	83	83	88	83	82
Rural Non-Farm	74	78	79	77	81	81	86	86
Farm	74	76	71	77	72	75	76	78
RACE								
White	78	77	78	84	82	85	NA	86
Non-White	62	75	74	82	75	85	NA	75

Source: Benson & Benson, Inc. Information supplied by S&H Corporate Research Department

19

Table 2

PERCENTAGES OF UNITED STATES ADULTS
WHO LIKE TRADING STAMPS AND AN ANALYSIS OF SAVERS
1959 TO 1966

PERCENTAGES OF ADULTS	1959	1960	1961	1962	1963	1964	1965	1966
Who Say They Like Stamps								
Women	82	82	78	79	81	76	86	80
Men	71	66	66	66	63	61	69	67
WHO SAVE STAMPS FOR REDEMPTION								
Women	79	79	78	86	83	85	87	85
Men	74	74	74	81	74	85	75	84
Age of Head of Household								
21 - 34	80	81	84	85	82			
35 - 49	80	78	78	89	86			
50 and Over	71	73	68	78	76			
Age of Married Adult								
18 - 34						85	84	86
35 - 44						88	84	89
45 - 54						90	85	89
55 Plus						83	80	83
Education*								
Grammar School	77	69	69	80	73	81	76	79
Any High School	77	79	79	87	84	87	85	86
Any College	75	82	76	82	80	83	85	86
S&H Regions								
East	77	73	74	83				
South Central	83	83	84	83				
Midwest	73	77	75	87				
West	76	86	81	85				
Northeast						87	87	91
South Central						84	86	85
East Central						85	82	84
North Central						81	79	79
Middle Atlantic							84	79
South Atlantic							84	90
Pacific						87	86	91

* 1959 to 1963 population over 25
1964 to 1966 population over 17.

SOURCE: Benson & Benson, Inc., Princeton. Information supplied by S&H Corporate Research Department.

like stamps have outnumbered 10:1 or more those who want them out-lawed. According to Tables 1 (Share of United States Households) and 2 (Share of Adults), stamps were saved for redemption by a majority of adults in every age group, in every territory, and in every socio-economic segment surveyed. "Generally speaking, women are more susceptible to the premium inducement than men," Sumner Slichter had observed about half a century before;[3] the tabulations show what this pattern has endured. But in the years 1959 to 1966, two-thirds of the men surveyed also gave the system their endorse-ment. The stamp medium provides articles wanted for the consumer's home or hobby. The appeal of the premiums runs the gamut from conspicuous consumption to charitable concern. Besides these practi-cal considerations, a number of social and psychological satisfactions arise from the saving process itself.

The housewife finds that the collecting of trading stamps has what Slichter called "neighborhood interest . . . for the interest of one per-son stimulates the interest of the others." To use an expression cur-rent fifty years later, "all the other girls are with it" and are showing off their gifts. Trading stamps are the stake at bridge parties, the donation to a local charity drive, and the topic of conversation. They are the inspiration for cartoonists and television gag writers, and they are used or mentioned in the most unexpected places. "To many peo-ple today," a Lutheran minister was quoted in a Christmas 1966 article in The Wall Street Journal, " 'redemption' means trading in your green stamps." "Green Stamps" was also the title of a jazz record. Stories about stamps are legion. Evidently, they appeal to the American sense of humor.

Yet trading stamps also project a serious appeal to the reflective shopper who feels an affinity for other housewives. As in any buyer-seller relationship, there inheres a conflict of interest between the two sides but a community of feeling among one's own. The same house-wife who may see no objection to getting something extra at the pos-sible expense of her supplier might react differently if it were at the expense of other shoppers. Because the bounty is given to all custom-ers on all purchases the system appeals to some housewives' sense of equity. She may regard selective price cuts or contests as discrimi-natory.

The trading stamp also gives its savers personal satisfactions. It appeals to the age-old pleasures of giving and receiving presents. More than 20% of all redemptions are for gifts to people outside the family.

In view of the familial neglect felt by some housewives everywhere, stamps also may function as a token of appreciation where appreciation is scarce. And merchandise expresses thanks and esteem more respectfully than money. It is easier to discuss the economic than the material aspects of stamps. "A small value in merchandise has more significance to the recipient than the same value in cash," declared Professor Haring in a talk before the Trading Stamp Institute. "A speaker, for example, can be highly gratified by an engraved pen and pencil set, although the cash involved (if presented coldly as cash only) might be considered completely inadequate." [9] The same is often true for the shopper who may regard stamps as her "reward" but price reductions as her "due." Moreover, since trading stamps are not money, the housewife can often use their redemption value on goods for which the husband may be unwilling to incur a financial expenditure.

The dual-currency aspect that is sometimes castigated as a complication makes the trading stamp convenient for the woman who does not maintain a set of books on her household expenditures. She may view stamps as having a separate source and a separate purpose from cash. The tokens are easily identified as a separate fund for upgrading one's home or for other postponable acquisitions. Their lack of liquidity keeps the saver steadfast in her objective—unlike money in the piggy bank, the stamps cannot be diverted for miscellaneous emergencies. Somehow, senses the harassed adult, money for those "wonderful gifts" pictured in stamp catalogs may never be spared. The assurance that this purchasing power will not be diverted to institutionally compelling outlays may relieve the tensions of a craving for indulgences.

At first glance the homemakers' illiquidity preference may seem irrational but, like some other behavior, it may be well motivated and understandable. "The major practice of present-day American consumers," explained Professor Katona, "of buying on installments and paying high interest charges even though cash is available or could be accumulated fairly soon . . . may be called 'super-rational' rather than irrational: it appears that many consumers take their own shortcomings into account (namely, that they would not save money if they were not pressured to save)." [10] Even the largest corporations resort to self-restrictions or illiquidity in order to achieve longer-range objectives: they may appropriate Retained Earnings or transfer Cash to a special-purpose Fund account.

One sees this same phenomenon operating elsewhere, for example in deferred employment benefits. Like trading stamps, pension and stock options are viewed as an extra—not the dominant motive for most employees but a powerful one if the more important employment conditions offered are alike. Pensions and stock options exert a particularly strong held on employee allegiance. Many of the conflicts engendered by stamps apply similarly to pension privileges.

In an article on stamps Professor Milton Friedman, president of the American Economic Association in 1967, is quoted as follows: "People are willing to pay people to make them, force them, to save."[11] In contrast to contractual accumulation plans (Christmas clubs, annuity policies) which Americans have substituted increasingly for cash, the stamp system entails no noticeable money outlay. Stamps are ordinarily not sold outright nor were tests of advancing them on credit successful. The trading stamp system is a process of building an irrevocable trust fund for transitory consumption. If the redemption merchandise is a part of the permanent-consumption assortment, a corresponding cash amount is released for the choice of either advancing the movement toward an assets equilibrium or adding a nonconforming enjoyment.

When all of the family's income (including the housewife's) is either committed or used for unavoidable family requirements, she misses the freedom of what used to be called "egg money" in the home—like a "cushion" in business budgeting—for truly discretionary deployment outside of established constraints. Cash saved on price reductions or cash earned on unexpected overtime is indistinguishable from other income and would often flow out for unexpected needs. But the cache of trading stamps is the housekeeper's own separate reward and prerogative. In the words of a Cleveland shopper: "If I saved a penny here and there on food, the savings would just disappear. The stamps you collect until you have enough to get something nice. And since it's extra, you don't have to be practical."[12] In technical terms, the marginal propensity to consume differs from the average.

In addition to the incentive in the form of a premium, saving itself provides a secondary reinforcement. From receipt to redemption, the process fits well with the modern American way of life which Houthakker and Taylor concluded is a "consumption pattern characterized mainly by habit formation."[13] Simply acquiring stamps is, for many people, almost as satisfying as the receipt of merchandise, in part because they connote the anticipation of getting valuable goods later on. "The housewife who has her attention fixed on the possibility of procuring a free cook book, radio, guitar, watch, or traveling bag," an economist explained 35 years ago, "has her buying attitudes aroused and stimulated by motives entirely different from those involved in the straight-forward purchase of her more or less prosaic household necessities."[14] Thus stamps impart to the shopping chore what men refer to as "the fun of the game" in their struggle for business. Just the act of filling books becomes a satisfying goal—about two-thirds of savers surveyed in 1966 felt such a sense of achievement. And as one book is filled, there is a feeling of urgency to start another.[15] The self-image of virtue during the saving-pasting-storing chore leads to a sense of self-satisfaction when the tokens are converted to a premium. The degree to which stamps satisfy the wants of some savers can perhaps be demonstrated in a confrontation with cash.

Stamps Versus Cash. There are hundreds of testimonials from enthusiastic as well as reluctant merchants to the effect that they have found stamps superior to price cuts in getting and holding patronage. At meetings of businessmen's organizations such as the Super Market Institute and the National Association of Retail Druggists, in interviews for trade publications such as *Progressive Grocer* and *Hardware Retailer*, merchants have celebrated or lamented the consumer's response in favor of the tokens. Even in the mid-1960's after enthusiasm for stamps had peaked, many retailers figured that if they discontinued them, enough consumers would defect so that no savings would be forthcoming. In fact, some retailers even felt that higher prices would have to result.

Although the following pages analyze a choice between stamps and cash, in practice the delineation is not so clear cut. Some stores are elegant, high-priced, and do not use stamps. Stores that are open at odd hours for the shopper's convenience may or may not subscribe to the system. Even among stores featuring discount prices, a 1964 study found, one-fifth gave trading stamps to their customers.[16] Thus it should be kept in mind that in the market place there is a continuum of pricing and promotional mixes.

A number of experiments and investigations have confirmed that many consumers prefer stamps over small amounts of cash. For example, in one research study the writers concluded: "The ability of stamps to sustain or even build sales in areas where customers could realize more immediate and sometimes greater savings by shopping on a price basis suggests that stamps and price cuts cannot be exactly equated. Each device has its own appeal, and stamps appeal to certain customers more than an equal or even greater inducement in the form of lower prices." [17]

This aspect of consumer behavior has been corroborated in a nation-wide study for the American Petroleum Institute.[18] Further, an article in *National Petroleum News* reported that gas stations in the Detroit and New Orleans areas charged stamp takers extra by having separate islands, one offering a cash price and the other offering stamps if the customer paid extra. In both cities, 75% of the customers elected to pay one cent or two cents more per gallon in order to get the stamps.[19] Such experiments are usually short-lived but new ones are reported frequently. In August and September of 1966, for instance, the King Soopers chain of grocery stores offered their customers a choice of either 1 stamp per ten-cent purchase or a 2% cash discount at the checkout. At first, customers favored stamps 3:1; by the time the experiment ended, more than 90% were taking the stamps.[20]

Other lines of trade in which prices are more difficult to compare due to greater merchandise heterogeneity experienced an even greater sales leverage from the consumer subsidy. "Most evidence available suggests that trading stamps—in the many ways they are used—have between three and five times as strong an effect on customer behavior as equivalent changes in price." [21]

Research on applesauce at Cornell University also confirmed the greater promotional power of stamps. Sales at the regular price of two cans for 33 cents (16½ cents per can) were contrasted with volume at a price cut of 2.2 cents per can and at an offer of 30 or 50 trading stamps per four cans. The costs to the stores of these offers were 2.2 cents for the price cut, 1.6 cents per can for 30 and 2.5 cents per can for 50 stamps. With the price cut and advertising, sales increased an average of eight times. With the stamp offers, on average, sales increased about 15 times. (Thirty pieces appeared to be as effective as 50.) Thus the stamp offers produced almost twice the impact for slightly lower cost.[22]

In 1963 approximately 55% of the persons interviewed in connection with the *Burgoyne Study of Supermarket Shoppers* stated that most people prefer to shop in a store giving trading stamps rather than an otherwise identical store that is 2% cheaper on all goods but does not disburse them.[23] The popularity has continued even though surveys indicate that slightly more than one-half of supermarket shoppers believe that stamps contribute to higher food prices.[24] This may reflect many shoppers' concurrent suspicion that prices would not come down (or stay down) if the stamps were discontinued. Rather, these shoppers may reason, other promotions of lower desirability will be substituted. Indeed, this is exactly what did happen in Kansas.

A market researcher who offered housewives a choice of one hundred stamps or twenty-five cents for returning a mail questionnaire reported that 58% of the respondents chose the tokens and 42% the coin.[25] But due to his small sample, the results are statistically not significant. More reliably, the research firm of Benson and Benson, Inc., which allows respondents to select cash or any brand of stamps, found that in 1963 when the offer was one dollar cash or four hundred stamps, 37% of the respondents chose cash and 62% chose stamps. (1% had no preference.) In 1965 a staff writer of *The Christian Science Monitor* interviewed "nearly one hundred New England retailers" as part of his background research for an article. "With not one exception, the dealers told stories of shoppers who would carefully count each stamp, fold them carefully, put them in their pockets, and then happily walk out, leaving several dollars in change lying on the counter."[26]

As on any issue, the verdict of the citizenry is not uniform. "Lower prices, supermarkets have learned, can lick trading stamps," headlined *Barron's*.[27] Emphasis on heavily advertised low prices enabled a seventeen-store chain in Michigan to drop a local stamp brand successfully[28] But many retailers note that a change-over requires very deep price cuts. Commenting on adverse profit results when stamps were dropped in supermarkets taken over by his firm, the chairman of Korvette, Inc., explained that "increased promotional expenses and sharp price reductions are both incurred during the withdrawal period."[29] Similarly, when Stop and Shop, Inc. defected, its earnings were substantially depressed before returning a year later to near pre-stamp levels, according to its chairman.

Certain inferences seem to be justified. First, merchants have decided that the ordinary volume of advertising, though heavy, is inadequate to have their message of lowered price tags penetrate. Apparently they feel that some consumers are not particularly alert to price reductions. Second, they do not fear that the consumer will notice subsequent price increases should they become necessary.

Most of the foregoing citations testify to the depth and breadth of pro-stamp attitudes. Many consumers regard stamps as more useful than equivalent amounts of currency but it is also a fact that some people dislike stamps and that a few oppose them vehemently. ". . . Not all customers respond in the same way—let alone in the same degree. For example, there is considerable evidence that many people who actually save trading stamps are hostile to trading-stamp companies because they don't believe they are really getting the stamps without extra charge; they are resentful because they believe the trading-stamp companies are trying to deceive them." [30]

Among some people the little gummed papers arouse a sense of mission to destroy them. Professor R. L. D. Morse has called upon the American Home Economics Association to "distinguish itself from the mass opinions and reflect a position which respects intelligence." [31] He stated that his committee's recommendation that trading stamps be legislated out of existence 'is not intended to represent necessarily the will of the majority of consumers."

Aside from intellectual disdain, stamps also engender emotional involvement. The nonsaver, especially, is likely to look upon any stamps that he happens to get as an imposition. There also is the practical side—are they worth an effort? Without a doubt, many Americans regard the gummed papers as a bother or they do not like to paste them into a saver book. These people resent the time involved in handling the stamps and they lack the time to visit a redemption center.

Ordinarily, most housewives enjoy shopping for department-store type of goods [32] but when women re-enter the labor force, time becomes especially precious. Also, in some households the extra wages may relegate the importance of the deferred discount until a new scale of living absorbs the extra income. The expansion in employment after 1963 may have been one reason for the drop-off in the holding power of stamps. Of greater importance is the likelihood that many people no longer much care one way or the other. They are the "situational" savers who take the stamp when it is freely available but would not miss it if it were discontinued.

There has also been a reaction from individuals who — alienated from the main stream of American life — reject anything popular. Moreover, there is no room for enterprise differentiation in certain extremist ideologies. But the frequency of the stamp-insistence observations, the persistence over nearly two decades, the variety of sources, the dispersion throughout the country, the recurrence in various types of shopping and nonshopping situations, all support the assertion that some consumers prefer stamps over equivalent amounts of cash or other promotions. This phenomenon can be explained by recourse to some established economic theories.

An Hypothesis of Stamp Preference. "The consumer," E. A. G. Robinson has pointed out, "may attach himself to a single producer, and refuse to transfer his custom to another, who offers the same product just a little cheaper . . . because the saving to be obtained from going to the alternative shop is less than the value of the time, or fare, or petrol, spent in going there." [33] Professor R. T. Norris formulated the concept that below a certain level of expenditure (which is different for each person), the individual deems an outlay relatively insignificant and unworthy of effort. Generally, the threshold at which attention to money starts will be higher the wealthier and the busier the individual is. [34] "Higher incomes," explains the Report of the National Commission on Food Marketing, "make consumers less willing to vary purchases in response to moderate price changes." [35]

Once it is posited that up to a certain amount a price differential is rationally ignored, it follows that unperceived, uncontrolled cash savings are not accounted for in the household's general stream of financial flows. Some consumers might try to capture such trifling amounts through piggy banks but there are problems of inflows and outflows. The shopper must remember to divest herself of the odd amount deemed to be a saving; each member of the family must repulse the urge to squander the cash or the pressure to merge it with the general fund. In the case of stamps, automatic receipt obviates the need to remember divestment and illiquidity prevents diversion. The point is that if, in the absence of stamps, price cuts could be sustained, many consumers would allow the small cash savings to disappear and at the same time they would lack the premiums. The same reasoning may apply to the seconds it takes to paste each receipt into saver books: such fleeting change of pace has no remunerative alternate.

If this interpretation is correct, it means that some consumers find stamps more functional than price cuts in the widening zone where stamps (a) are sufficiently plentiful to deliver value and (b) are viewed as alternatives to trifles. It appears (a) that for many consumers the post-1950 rate of receipt is adequate to sustain interest and (b) that for some, the stamp in terms of its cash and time values is a petty by-product. Between the Korean and the Vietnamese conflicts, the average transaction in a supermarket trended from three dollars to five dollars which corresponds to about six cents to nine cents in cost of stamps; the average sale of gasoline has been even less. (Food and gasoline retailers account for about 80% of all stamp usage).

By way of digression it may be noted that in a case involving disbursement on fair-traded toothpaste, a court considered the effect of trading stamps to be *de minimis*. Computing that the purchase of a "long lifetime" supply would entitle a saver to redeem his stamps for merchandise worth $1.75 and adjusting for stampless sales, the court concluded "the "infraction charged appears to be still more trifling than above indicated." [36]

Summary. Although the foregoing does not purport to be a complete explanation of consumers' behavior relative to stamps in grocery stores and gasoline stations during the heyday of the gummed subsidy, perhaps enough aspects have been mentioned to suggest its dimensions. The appeal is at once obvious and subtle, amusing and serious, rational and cultural, psychological and social.

At first consumers apparently accepted stamps as a commission for prompt payment or for buying efforts. Many savers came to identify the gratuity as *incremental* purchasing power; this may help to explain why stamps are often prized more highly than equivalent cash on which routine commitments have prior claims. When each individual receipt of stamps is small, the financial equivalent can be rationally disregarded. When the receipts are frequent they serve as reminders, and saving is worth while. This demand for the fractional merchandise certificates including the preference over paltry amounts of cash seems to be consistent with widely accepted economic theories of consumer behavior. But all demand above the subsistence level contains an ingredient of fashion, and a prediction of the course of taste is outside the realm of economics.

If any one motive had to be singled out, this observer would nominate the consumer's realization that the stamps' illiquidity reserves their conversion for wanted merchandise which in a pure monetary economy would not be purchased. Instead of defying reason or logic, perhaps the consumer's enchantment with trading stamps should indeed be termed super-rational.

Consumer insistence has wrought many changes in food retailing and elsewhere. Supermarkets, the major source of stamps for most savers, are one place where these effects may be examined.

CHAPTER IV

SUPPLY THROUGH SUPERMARKETS

"The most strategic aspect of American production and marketing is endeavors of large enterprises or of organized, voluntary groupings of small enterprises to gain and hold the favor of the ultimate consumer . . ." declares a distinguished expert in industrial organization economics. "In the background always is the actual or potential new product or service to threaten the position of established brands; in the foreground always is advertising." [1]

Supermarkets have become the prototype and main pillar of the role played in this connection by the trading stamp system. (Other types of contracting retailers — referred to in this work as associate accounts — will be considered in the next chapter). This chapter is devoted to an examination of the hypothesis that the dynamic structure of retailing itself forces the stores to accommodate consumer demand by enlisting such tools as trading stamps.

THE WHEEL OF RETAILING

Many forms of retailing that originally achieved mass appeal through low-margin austerity have retained their position in the mass market by stressing nonprice competition over price competition. Successive cycles of this phenomenon, which McNair has called "the wheel of retailing" [2] can be observed for department stores, mail order firms, variety stores, food chains and supermarkets, and discount houses — to name some.

Theoretical Perspective. It is the later stage of such a cycle which is of interest here. It is marked, as McNair points out, by the emergence of evcess capacity as more and more dealers join the new merchandising method. Other experts call attention to the changes of the "mass" market; the provision of services must keep pace with the increasing sophistication in tastes of the consumer segment that patronizes the store. [3]

Economists also have commented on the effect of such changes in the competitive situation as well as in the market itself. "The ordinary unit of retail selling, the shop, is limited in size by the local market, and seldom, it would appear, reaches its optimum scale." [4] This implies chronic inefficiency that only a superior pulling power can relieve. Thus the instability that appears to characterize retailing is not surprising. Confined to a limited shopping area, the established retailer has what Stigler calls "unavoidable excess capacity."[5] The retailer strives for better use of his plant by increasing services which lead to higher gross margins that attract price-cutting innovators — who repeat the cycle.

Nonprice competition may enable the aggressive retailer to stay ahead of his rivals. "The high cost of selling may be, paradoxically, at the same time a source of economy, making the already large firm more efficient than the smaller firm, and a cost of growth which makes it unprofitable for the small firm to grow up to its most efficient size."[6] Small retailers may match a price cut but not an advertising expenditure. First, the outlay for advertising is speculative and second, the smaller store may lack the facilities to recoup it. And, as Penrose notes, there is a vast difference between a price cut and a sales effort. The former leaves the seller's name insignificant; the latter features his name and paves the way for a close relationship between seller and buyer.[7] Indeed the retailer's survival hinges on his ability to cultivate goodwill in the sense of Lord Eldon's dictum, "the probability that customers will return to the old stand."

In the battle of business to meet the direct and derived demand of consumers the weakest contender is probably the intermediary with homogeneous goods, like the retailer of food and gasoline. Ease of entry and deceptive simplicity of operation make the retailing of staples a form of disguised unemployment for the newcomers who invest some cash, a captive labor force, and unrealistic hopes.

While a policy of prices that are reasonable in the retailer's market is necessary, it is not sufficient. If his merchandising assortment or mode of operation does not distinguish him, the vendor must devise a different strategy that will attract and retain patronage. Lest the strategy be ephemeral, the action must be something that cannot be readily equalled. Ordinarily, this rules out price reduction alone because there usually will be someone or some ones who will match the "spoiler." This retaliation is possible because the supply functions of supermarkets often are similar. Lest the strategy be speculative, the action must be something that entails no outlay unless a sale takes place. Usually this rules out an extraordinary advertising campaign. Virtually all large stores advertise and could step up their expenditures in retaliation to a rival's saturation policy. More likely, it would not be necessary since diminishing marginal productivity should accrue from a store's protracted strategy of advertising escalation. Thus the exclusive device should combine the drawing power of a price cut and the lasting persuasiveness of a successful campaign.

Although it is not a panacea, there is a technique of "semi-price competition"[8] that under the described market conditions meets most of these specifications: the trading stamp. In many cases it even surpasses the specifications. Sometimes it falls short. It must always be remembered that consumers are heterogeneous and no single strategy will satisfy all.

Historical Background of Retail Services. Use of premiums and other nonprice promotions developed hand-in-hand with radical changes in retailing itself. The idea for a premium system was an ingenious triumph over adversity. In 1850 Benjamin Talbot Babbitt tried to sell laundry soap in individually paper-wrapped pieces instead of in bulk. When his idea was rebuffed, he printed coupons on the wrapping. After this modification his brand enjoyed prompt acceptance. The housewife could get an attractive color lithograph for twenty-five coupons. Thus the premium system provided for continuity of brand allegiance.

Due to its success the idea of coupons had many imitators, some of whom enlarged on it in important ways. For example, coupon-giving retailers and manufacturers provided premium lists, allowing customers to choose from a number of items. By that time, however, the more important pressures on retailing were exerted by the growth of large department stores, the spreading of small chain stores, and the popularity of mail order firms.

Of these, department stores grew to pamper city women with a wide and orderly selection of merchandise and a multitude of services. The early chains, which were very small stores with a specialized line of goods, used their concentration of buying power and their efficiency to offer customers lower prices. These two types of retailers both were mass marketers serving the increasingly populous American cities. As their size and diversity of goods outgrew the single proprietor, many managerial activities had to be delegated which, in turn, required a one-price policy.[9] In effect, they surrendered the flexibility of adjusting to the individual prospect — a milestone in the still-continuing trend of depersonalization in retailing. Their rapid growth, which was much faster than total income, implies that they diverted substantial trade from established shopkeepers.[10] Considerable ingenuity in sales promotion and advertising helped bring this diversion. In this approach they were joined in the 1870's by a third type of merchant — the large mail order house. This nonstore retailer offered a wide variety of merchandise and featured liberal guarantee or return policies. Its acceptance and growth accustomed many consumers in rural areas and elsewhere to selecting their wants from a catalog with trustworthy descriptions and authentic illustrations.

As these retailers moved from inception and growth through price appeals to nonprice appeals, they tried many devices. Advertisements were widely used although they had limitations and frustrations. For example, the messages did not reach many of the immigrants and illiterates who were an increasing part of the mass market. As a further example, "it was not until 1911 that the New York *Herald* would accept Lane Bryant's first advertisement for maternity dresses." [11] One frequently used tactic to overcome these obstacles was the use of premiums. As one economist later explained: "The most important psychological and economic fact in premium-giving is that it diverts the buyer's attention from the thing which is being *bought* to the thing which is being *given*." [12] Premiums were "used with apparent advantage by mail order houses, chain stores, and department stores. . . ." another economist reported. [13]

It was against this background that the trading stamp, used in America since the early 1890's, enjoyed wider and wider retailer acceptance. It appears a logical outgrowth of premium-giving, catalog use, and retailer needs for promotional devices. The accumulated experiences with premiums, the intense competition at the retail level, and the burgeoning demand beyond basic necessities had indeed set the stage. As Carl Menger has pointed out, new forms of money appear in response to changes in economic circumstances. [14] And it is not surprising that American trading stamps originated in the institution that specializes in catering to women — the department store.

By the late 1890's the trading-stamp business was dominated by independent specialists. "The development of trading stamps is a significant bit of merchandising history," noted Leverett S. Lyon. "This is partly because it changed the method of premium-giving; even more because it reflected the rise of a new middleman in the premium business — the premium company; and most of all, perhaps, because it represented a shift from the manufacturer to the dealer as the center of the buyer's interest." [15] It appears that trading stamps thrive when a large sector dealing with the consumer needs to motivate him with an extra incentive — for prompt payment, for patronage, or whatever — and when they are widely enough available to put premiums within reach.

Application of Wheel of Retailing to Supermarkets. Grocery stores account for about one-quarter of all United States retail volume[16]. They are the infrastructure of the latest vigor of trading stamps. The giving of something extra with retail food sales is as traditional as the baker's dozen.

In the early 1870's the Great Atlantic and Pacific Tea Company systematically gave "premiums, consisting of glassware and crockery, to consumers;"[17] other tea and coffee companies followed suit. Prior to World War I, the A. & P. was the largest single user of S & H Green Stamps;[18] other large users of stamps were the Acme Tea Company of Philadelphia and Brill Brothers in New York.[19] Apparently, the "quite atomistic" structure of food retailing then prevailing[20] was conducive to the use of premiums. Thereafter, the structure of food retailing changed rapidly and as the industry moved through other stages of the cycle it moved away from gift-giving.

The chain stores embarked on a policy of aggressive expansion, including vertical and horizontal integration and predatory price-cutting. In 1920 grocery chains supplied less than 3% of the market but by 1930 five large chains had captured about 25%.[21] Yet entry into retailing remained easy, even as survival became more difficult. During the Great Depression, the number of grocery stores increased 80%.[22] Since 1939 there has been a steady attrition of the "mom-and-pop" stores. The Great Depression also saw the beginnings of the supermarket.

"The first true self-service supermarket did not appear until the early 1930's when King Cullen opened his first market in an abandoned Long Island garage with empty ginger-ale cases for display tables."[23] By 1940 there was one supermarket per about 5,700 families; still an unusual store featuring low prices and excluding such frills as trading stamps. After World War II the construction of supermarkets resumed, making up for lost time. In the wake of the postwar surge, supermarkets lost their local uniqueness; "overstoring" (meaning an excess of stores) became the operators' main problem. And quickly the wheel turned from aggressive price competition to forms of nonprice competition.

In each trading area more than half of the volume came to be supplied by one or two very large supermarket chains plus a few local chains and large independents, leaving the "very numerous small grocers" — in Bain's terminology — as a "competitive fringe." Accordingly, the focus of the supermarkets' rivalry changed from traditional small stores to other supermarkets, and they curried favor with the increasingly exacting shopper.

Supermarkets added such shopping comforts as more convenient locations; wider aisles; broader assortments; additional check-out and express lanes; larger parking space; longer store hours; new departments such as bakery, delicatessen, and prescription drug sections; improved atmosphere provided by airconditioning, music, restrooms, special lighting effects, murals, automatic doors; more equipment for meats, frozen foods, shelf display; extra services such as check-cashing and parcel pick-up stations or free deliveries to parking lot; increases in advertising — all pushing on their Depression-born low-cost policy. The luxuriant trend is continuing, along with a counter-trend of renewed interest in discount foodstores. 1463265

These expensive services satisfied the apparent wants of the consumer but they failed to relieve the industry from the threat of excessive competition: like the price reductions of the 1930's, the luxury provisions were imitated and escalated. All of this frenetic and expensive activity, and more, could not assure the operator absorption of his idle capacity. The continuing influx into the trade — newcomers who could exploit the latest changes in living patterns and adopt the latest innovations in retailing technology — shifted the established merchants' demand curves to the left. The new entrants were another element that pushed up unit costs. "It is a case where an increased supply means higher instead of lower prices," as Chamberlin theorized.[24]

Moreover, the supermarkets added retailers' brands, specialty foods, beauty aids, all of which increased consumers' choice — and raised margins (gross profits as a percentage of sales). Hence it is not surprising that the margins of retail food corporations rose throughout most of the 1940's,[25] about a decade before trading stamps became prominent. Similarly, the large chains like Safeway, Kroger, and American Stores, posted rising margins[26] also for about a decade before they introduced stamps. But the many variables that determine reported food stores' expenses and profits preclude their analysis in this book. The point is that long before the widespread adoption of stamps, a trend of increasing margins had been embedded in the food trade. And after the mass conversion to stamps in the mid-1950's, the discussion will anticipate at this point, gross profits of the three very light users—The Great Atlantic and Pacific Tea Company,

Safeway Stores, and Jewel Tea Company — rose much more than of the other food chains who had become regular users of stamps.[27]

But to resume the wheel of retailing, by the 1950's the cycle had developed to where the supermarket industry found itself engulfed by an increasing number of large stores, suppliers with presold brands, employees in aggressive unions, and a loss of personal contact with its customers. The merchants' situation was relatively inflexible.

Supermarkets are not sufficiently divisible to cope with overstoring. The hourly and daily distribution of patronage is highly skewed, yet all departments must be in operation when the store is open. By its presence, the supermarket enhances the commercial uses of the surroundings. Thus horizontal expansion is blocked by unavailability of contiguous land. Unfamiliarity of consumers with multilevel food stores has precluded vertical expansion. Temporal expansion is regulated by laws such as cover maximum daily working hours, overtime wages, and Sunday selling. "Once a distributor has decided where to put a store, and how big to build it," concludes the McKinsey-General Foods Study, "he has pretty well set at least the range of its future profits." [28]

Nor is their plant highly adaptable. Property taxes, insurance premiums, rents, and other expenses tend to be fixed costs. The secular rise in operating costs after World War II had no direct relationship to physical volume. Retail workers' unions increasingly succeeded in restricting (a) managerial prerogatives, such as the functional and temporal deployment of store personnel and (b) marketing practices, such as the free use of manufacturers' missionary salesmen for building displays and stocking shelves. Supermarkets did succeed, however, in substituting various kinds of equipment for labor and in reducing sales-clerking. But this efficiency move also intensified their depersonalization.

The loss of individuality reinforced the supermarket's image of a formal business, carrying the same brands as the other supermarkets, offering the same conveniences, and charging just as much. In less than two decades the supermarket had become a comfortable and commonplace store to the shopper; an enmeshed and exposed firm to the merchant.

Resistance to Stamps. Although some food merchants such as Worth Markets in Fort Worth, Texas, were using trading stamps in the 1930's, there were no important repercussions until King Soopers in Colorado and others experimented with the gift during the time of the Korean conflict. In a depression, customers do not receive enough of the fractional coupons to react dramatically. Behavior is conditioned by the struggle for subsistence. But two decades after the Great Depression, the preconditions for the growth of the stamp system were extraordinarily auspicious: (1) consumers wanted many goods and bought from many sources and (2) retailers were struggling to achieve a form of enterprise differentiation attuned to the times.

Nevertheless, almost every major food chain fought bitterly to escape what most retail executives regard as an albatross. The president of National Tea Company is quoted in *Fortune* as follows: "'We fought stamps with everything we had before we capitulated. But women believe in them. They'll leave their change on the counter, but not their stamps.[29] The Kroger Company had the same experience as National Tea, according to The *Wall Street Journal.* "We fought them by cutting prices; we gave away hosiery, dishes, and dolls. We used every gimmick known — and still the stamp stores took sales away from us. We couldn't fight them, so we joined them," explained Kroger's president.[30]

Business leaders who acted on a model of price emphasis had much cause for regret. When Lingan Warren was president of Safeway Stores, his organization incurred enormous amounts of revenue reductions and expenses. Besides price cuts, Warren's Safeway employed tape register plans, antistamp advertising, and other antistamp actions.[31] Warren's successor announced that a million dollars awaits the man who offers a sound idea to get the supermarket industry out of the system.[32]

Among major retailers the longest holdout was The Great Atlantic and Pacific Tea Company, whose president reportedly called stamps "a drag on civilization" shortly before his company, too, surrendered to consumers' insistence. Some of the spokesmen of pharmacists and gasoline retailers have frequently even used more colorful language but their vigorous antistamp lobbying presentations are replete with unintentional testimonials for the power of stamps. It seems safe to conclude that after the Korean conflict the mass adoption of stamps by retailers of staples was a free market's adaptation to the general consumer mood.

STAMPS AT THE SUPERMARKET — FOUR STAGES

"Supermarkets which first used trading stamps in the early 1950's benefited from substantial increased volume."[33] By 1956, the Super

Market Institute reported, 40% of its members were then dispensing the gift.[34] Another survey about the same time[35] revealed that four out of five stamp-using supermarkets had enjoyed a sales increase, and that the average gain for all stores was 21%. Incidentally, these reports of sales rises confirm how prevalent the idle capacity had been. After trading stamps were introduced, volume spurts from 15 to 40% were common. But consumer reaction was by no means uniform; market conditions as well as people vary. It is possible, however, to generalize a trading-stamp sequence in store merchandising.

After generic demand has been developed, the first stores to introduce strongly supported brands of trading stamps will reap the greatest benefits. If successful, the premium-coupon will bring hefty sales gains. In the second stage, it stabilizes patronage at a higher rate of the retailer's capacity. At the third stage the merchant fears that he will lose volume if he relinquishes the medium. Disassociation from stamps ends the program. This sequence may be interrupted by competitive moves; for example, a rebound from stage three to stage one is possible in the wake of an important rival's defection from stamps. Conversely, a reluctant adoption followed by deficient merchandising of stamps may position the new user immediately into stage three. Many variations on this pattern will occur in practice.

Stimulation. The retailer who adopts trading stamps expects many things from them, but the stamp's primary function for the supermarket is to attract and hold customers. In view of the demand inelasticity faced by the food industry one may well wonder where the reported sales increases come from. It appears that many sources are tapped.

The market area can be widened. According to a study by the Stanford Research Institute,[36] stamp savers travel further to buy their groceries than nonsavers do. Shopping by car, the family purchasing agent can lengthen her selection radius without undue strain. Apparently the gift differentiates the retailer enough to induce the extra effort. A survey for *Look* magazine[37] corroborates a stamp-related market extension. In addition to widening the user's market, the gift may deepen it by motivating savers to concentrate their purchases at the stamp-giving store.

Growth can occur at the expense of smaller stores. The United States Department of Agriculture cited findings that supermarkets and superettes gained relatively more than small stores from the use of trading stamps.[38] An important variable is the size of the slack.

Although a small store has the advantage that a relatively large sales increase encroaches very little on competitors, the supermarket has the scale which enables it to service a huge influx of business. Thus stamps may have accentuated the exit of extramarginal firms.

The increase can also be at the cost of other supermarkets. Most areas can absorb less than a handful of strong brands of trading stamps. Hence association with a popular brand is important to the merchant. Of course, the early joiner can usually select the best vehicle and its continuing support will give him a lasting advantage. A successful conversion to stamps typically is aligned with other changes (such as longer store hours and broader product assortments) for a fuller exploitation of the revenue-augmenting instrument. A broader product offering can raise the total amount checked out at each trip. One-stop shopping thus has boosted the stake in the battle for the customer. Since stamps become increasingly useful to the saver as he receives more, he is likely to focus his trade at a supermarket that furnishes his brand.

Another function that many supermarket chains expect stamps to perform is to wedge into new markets. The movement of consumers to the suburbs after the Korean conflict accelerated the demand for new retail stores. An established stamp brand may reduce the cost of new operations by eliminating the losses of a lengthy shake-down period and by reducing the risk of eventual failure. The trading stamp attracts volume from the start. Confidence in the gift's ability to hold volume may have influenced managements to build large, optimal-size stores instead of a series of small, less efficient, but also less risky, units. The same reasoning may apply to expansion into settled areas.

However reluctant to embrace the system, a supermarket has many inducements and pressures to do so. As rivals observe a stamp user's success, they have to retaliate. They can lower prices, institute new promotions, offer extra services, or adopt a competitive brand of trading stamp.

Stabilization. When many stores of the same type have adopted rival stamp brands the vehicle's power to amass a disproportionate increase in sales is neutralized, and Stage 2 of the trading-stamp sequence is underway. Stabilization in a market can occur because one or more users are satisfying a limited consumer interest in stamps and rivals find that the expense of introducing other brands is not warranted. But in the 1960's the more frequent case was a strong consumer wish for stamps. Additional adoptions heightened people's interest in them [39] but whittled away the rate of extra gains that users had enjoyed in Stage 1.

From the merchant's point of vantage the retail market is plentifully supplied with stamps but the consumer is far from sated. During this period of proliferation, the stamp's main contribution is to hold patronage at the increased level achieved in the prior stage. Even if market share is static over a period of time, a supermarket will be adding many new shoppers. It will be replacing the customers that in the ordinary course of events inevitably are lost. Americans are mobile; people change addresses at the annual rate of 20%. Time takes its toll of loyal customers, and newly formed households must be attracted. Thus there always is an element of Stage 1 with its emphasis on the gift's sales-expansion function.

A franchised or protected stamp confers upon its user a differential advantage. The cross-elasticity of demand between different brands of stamps is very low. Therefore a supermarket that meets the shopper's primary requirements (price, quality) can, through its stamp program, cultivate a lasting preference for its establishment. The trade retainer aspect of the gift reduces customer turnover, with a corresponding reduction in operating risks and wastes. When patronage is more predictable, retailers are in a better position to cater to their clientele. The quantity and assortment of their offerings, the scheduling of personnel, and the provision of various services can be efficiently attuned to the preferences of the core of steady customers. The loyal patrons contribute to a store atmosphere in which they feel comfortable.

The routinization of relationships brought about by the stamp has particular appeal to food chains. Weekly creation and conduct of suitable special promotions can be an enormous problem in internal administration and in coordination on both the supply and demand sides, with severe burdens on management and other resources. A strong stamp obviates the high costs of such a continuous round of new excitements.

Affiliation to the same brand by associate accounts (fuel dealers, dry cleaners, — in the past decade, probably every type of retailer has tried stamps) is an important external economy to the grocery retailers. Its wider availability makes his brand more effective, without encroaching on his volume. An entrenched stamp protects the user from forays into his area. To the extent that this is true, trading stamps retard what could be an even higher rate of entry into the supermarket trade.

In this stabilization phase, many users give extra stamps to level out the utilization of the plant. And there are several additional reasons why stamp-disbursing retailers practice this economic discrimination even though some issuers discourage it. Bonus stamps may speed the disposal of excess inventories or move a manufacturer's feature, the vendors perhaps defraying the promotional cost. In the 1966 Benson & Benson survey, 19% of the respondents stated that they checked their newspaper for bonus stamp offers before their last shopping trip. Or the supplemental quantity may call the consumer's attention to a new product, and induce him to try it. Sometimes, response was spectacular. For example, the Cornell University Agricultural Experiment Station ran a controlled experiment on frozen cherries. When 50 extra stamps were given with each can, sales per store increased about 10 times. With preferential placement of the cherries or an advertisement in addition to the stamps, volume rose even more.[40]

Besides, the use of extra stamps in lieu of temporary price changes may be quite efficient. A price change requires the re-pricing of all goods on the shelves, and the notification of all personnel concerned with marking the stocks and with checking out merchandise. A day or two later, all goods then on the shelves must once again be re-priced and the personnel notified accordingly. Inevitably, some stocks will remain with as many as three price markings; some may be overlooked in one of the re-pricing operations. A lot of effort, confusion, and possible ill-will can be avoided by giving bonus stamps instead of conducting multiple re-pricing operations. Beyond that, stamps may be more persuasive. As has been shown in Chapter III, the gummed tokens have often been more effective than a price cut.

Small price reductions may be ignored by consumers; large ones invite retaliation by competitors. Selective price cuts attract the least desired type of customer, called "cherry-picker." They discriminate in favor of the few who want the featured goods. A one-year test at Macy's revealed that loss leaders bring losses — but no offsetting sales of other goods at regular prices. Many merchants found that an active stamp program superimposed upon a reputation for everyday low prices (including the specialing cycle customary in food retailing) was the key to maintaining high volume, even if competitors had other stamp brands.

On the supermarket's demand side, stamps are a countervailing power against the market dominance of processors. "Dealers wish to have the good-will of the consumer attached to them — not to the manufacturer's goods, because they fear that if the manufacturer gains the good-will of the consumer he will be able to reduce the dealer's margin of profit." [41] Thus the enterprise differentiation can be functional in three directions: forward, horizontal, and backward. Accordingly, many retailers who have employed trading stamps ten or more years—much of the time under conditions of stamp stabilization — find that the gift continues to fit their financial and operational mix.

As a trade retainer, stamps have a comparative advantage and lack close substitutes. There is virtually no waste of promotional dollars. In contrast, most advertising messages are not noted by the majority of the audience. Among those who remember them, ill-will may be incurred if the advertised goods are not available. Coordination of advertising and supply is very difficult, especially in the smaller branches of a chain. Advertising is, of course, essential to the modern supermarket — an estimated 38% of all housewives check newspapers and circulars for prices — but few managers would rely on it unaided by other promotional tools. An efficient promotional mix for a supermarket may include advertising, stamps, and other tactics so that the intangible and tangible appeals reinforce each other.

Nationally, the percentage of savers may be in the 80's but for any particular stamp-disbursing supermarket it is likely to be higher. Nearly every customer participates and shares the usufruct. Thus the medium is highly efficient.

Saturation. Yet there is no assurance of a permanent equilibrium. Stamps are efficient to the saver but not to the supplier who is at Stage 3 of his stamp sequence, saturation, when they may or may not be effective. If all major competitors have them, if they no longer attract additional customers or even hold old ones . . . if they are not performing the marketing functions required of them, trading stamps have many disadvantages. It is always difficult to credit stamps for all their contributions because they are rarely independent of other market happenings but at Stage 3 of the model the evidence is particularly inconclusive. The retailer weighs the pros and cons, hoping for a clearcut signal from the patrons. On the one hand, the user has built up a following that is tied to the gift; on the other hand, he must give the vouchers with every sale, regardless of whether or not they are really essential to consummate that particular transaction.

The same medium that protects the middleman against the consumers' insistence on presold goods and manufacturers' policies of low margins is, itself, the ultimate in presold goods. The retailer must pay for the stamp and then bestow it on his customers without explicit reimbursement. This promotional service is not cheap; nor can its opportunity cost be ignored. According to the leading stamp company, a typical supermarket with annual sales of $1,200,000 could, in lieu of S & H stamps, use at the same cost such tools as an additional page of newspaper advertising every two weeks, a one-minute early-evening television spot commercial twice a week, or other tactics listed on Table 3. Again, the merchant may watch wistfully the excitement generated by his competitors' "long-shot" sweepstakes, which reportedly entail one-eighth the cost of stamps.[42]

Paradoxically, one of the features that makes stamps effective with consumers also is a cause of their resentment by merchants. Stamps are a ubiquitous reminder in the store whereas exposure to advertising is fleeting. After the manager authorizes advertising he can free his mind for other decisions. Nor does he linger over his accounting reports. But the process of incurring expenses for stamps is in constant evidence. There may be delays and disputes at the checkout, loss or theft of stamps, floor space for catalogs and saver books, displays for signs and streamers — as well as a portion of advertising linage devoted to stamps. The actual dollar outlay for these annoyances is relatively minor, but their visibility is high.

The franchised store is vulnerable to creative merchandising by non-stamp competitors. They can customize promotions for special events, for various motives, for sheer novelty, but continuous cost of the stamp does not brook such alternatives. "The primary disadvantage of stamps is that the merchant is committed for a long period of time, and is denied the flexibility of moving in and out of other types of promotions which can be very effective for a few weeks," explained Paul J. Cupp in a letter to the author. Mr. Cupp is chairman of the board, Acme Markets, Inc., a very large chain which in the mid-1960's continued trading stamps at most of its units, withdrew stamps from some, and introduced stamps in others — all in the same region. At Stage 3 such selective moves are not unusual.

The correct decision on trading stamps depends on a correct interpretation of consumer tastes and reactions. When the energizing influence of the gift wanes, many of the elements that can help make it productive have the opposite effect. This is the stopping point from the consumer's point of view: he is ready for a change. The established families may have filled their needs for the types of goods listed in stamp catalogs, and the interest in premiums may be

Table 3

WAYS IN WHICH A TYPICAL U.S. SUPERMARKET* CAN TRY AT EQUAL COST† TO ATTRACT CONSUMER PATRONAGE

1. Give trading stamps worth to consumers (if S&H):
   A. At discount store prices $25,000
   B. At department store prices $28,750

2. Do additional advertising:

   A. An additional page of newspaper advertising every two weeks in a typical metropolitan area.

   B. A one-minute early-evening TV spot commercial twice a week in a typical U.S. metropolitan area.

   C. Two radio spots, a day, at prime time, in a typical U.S. metropolitan area.

   D. A monthly circular mailed to every household in its trading area.

3. Increase the number of store personnel by one-fourth so that consumers receive more or faster service when they shop.

4. Offer phone orders and delivery on orders of $15 and up, *provided* no more than 10% of the customers take advantage of the offer.

5. Offer charge-account service *provided* no more than one-third of the business is done on this basis.

6. Stay open to serve customers 40% more hours (an extra 28 hours per week, or 97 rather than 69).

7. Use chance drawing-type promotions:
   A. Give one new Buick every two months to the customer with a lucky number.
   B. Give a "lucky" silver dollar each week to one of every 14 customers.

8. Cut prices across the board by 2%, by giving a 2% discount at the cash register on the total bill. (This provides a saving to consumers of only a dime on the average supermarket transaction of about $5, not enough to excite many shoppers.)

9. Reduce a few prices spectacularly below cost—for example, reduce by one-half the normal shelf price of sugar, ice cream, soap, coffee, and cookies. (This would reward a few customers handsomely and might also create for some shoppers the illusion of broad-scale cut prices.)

* A "typical" supermarket is one with sales of $1.2 million per year.

† $23,000 a year.

Source: S&H Corporate Research Department.

44

confined to new households. The pasting may suddenly appear burdensome or the consumer may show other signs of fatigue. The articulate foes of stamps may boycott the supermarket. One-sixth of America's households eschew stamps and an unknown percentage of the savers is apathetic. Consumer tastes are not only diverse but also volatile. Hence the revenue impact of stamps varies and is of uncertain duration. Consumers constantly need new stimulations.[48] In America's dynamic market the long run may be tomorrow. It does not take much to arouse the retailer's suspicion that maybe it is he — not the consumer — who is perpetuating the tax on his receipts.

Beyond the saturation point the cost of the stamps, itself, makes the user vulnerable to competition. He can be undersold. Geared to the stamp-effectiveness of stages 1 and 2, the retailer finds that his store is uneconomical to operate at Stage 3 when consumer response is erratic. Stamps may originally have contributed to a higher volume level serviceable partly by the plant's existing scale and partly by rises in variable costs. A drop in volume will not only leave the fixed costs intact but a ratchet effect will tend to freeze the upward-variable costs as well. Under ordinary circumstances the retailer will hardly couple a defection from stamps with a reduction in store hours or curtailment of merchandise stocks but it could be an effective move for dramatic impact.

Moreover, saturation is a strategic time for harassment by anti-stamp laws and anti-stamp investigations. But the risks of a misreading of the public mind deter a precipitate defection.

The decision is not a matter of majority rule. In the first place, customer votes should be weighted by average purchase—which is difficult to ascertain. Second, direct inquiries into consumers' attitudes toward trading stamps have been found to elicit misleading responses, imposing a validity-handicap on an informal survey of dubious reliability. Third, the results must be interpreted with extreme caution. If a survey indicates that 80% of the customers would continue to shop in the same store even if it dropped stamps and 20% would transfer to a stamp-user, an astute interpretation is that stamps must be continued. Who can afford to lose 20% of his customers?[44] The converse paradox would arise, of course, if the survey question had been phrased: "Will you transfer your patronage elsewhere because your store continues to give stamps?" If 80% answered no and 20% yes, the same reasoning as before would dictate that stamps be dropped.

The retailer's dilemma at Stage 3 is virtually inscrutable. If the data could be adduced, game theory might be employed. But "the best measurements of marginal cost have more than a 1% error." [45] The retailer's task is to weigh the likely cost savings and revenue opportunities from various mixes of price and promotional tactics, considering not only the reaction of his customers but also his competition. If the user relinquishes the stamp, his former brand becomes available to competitors. On paper, the closer to break-even the alternatives seem to be, the more inconclusive will be the financial projections. In the market, the efficacy of stamps is often tested by consumer surveys or experimental stores, but the Delphic nature of the answers renders them a tenuous basis for decision-making. Thus at the end of Stage 3 the final determination is a function of economics, emotion, and intuition.

Separation. Merchants who have decided to drop stamps have experienced diverse reactions. In some cases, nothing much happened. Others faced a vociferous protest. Although the marketing procedures appropriate for such a change-over are outside the scope of this book, a comment is relevant on the economic implication of one practice: the selling of stamps. [46] When a store discontinues stamps and cuts prices, the consumer, of course, finances the price reduction to the extent of the redemption-merchandise value. But the immediate loss is much greater because the stamps lacking toward a premium always have higher than aliquot values. Hence it is understandable why people who would under ordinary circumstances not knowingly part with cash for stamps are willing to do so when the supermarket stops giving them.

Store strategies in the wake of defection have varied. Some ex-users have converted to a discount-style operation, some have adopted contests, some personalized their relations with customers, and so on and so forth — some reverted to stamps. It is not always clear from summary reports subsequent to stamp decisions how much of a chain's volume changes are attributable to stamps and how much to other actions such as addition or discontinuation of branch stores.

While some stores have defected successfully, others who tried alternatives found them lacking. A senior vice president of Safeway Stores credited Bonus Bingo or other types of promotional games for "almost one-half" of its sales gain in early 1966. [47] But in November of that year the chain's chairman announced that Safeway would be "out of the game business by the first week of January." He added that "many Safeway divisions would reluctantly stay with trading stamps, at least for the time being."[48] Of two New York regional food chains that dropped stamps in 1965, one reported a minor rise and the other a minor reduction in sales. These two latter chains sustained heavy declines in profit, which their executives attributed to the change-over from trading stamps but felt would be temporary.[49] A combination of price and personalization brought a reported sales gain of 50% to a four-store company several months after it discontinued stamps.[50] But another enterprise of comparable size reinstated stamps within a year after it discontinued them, except that for one of its units its old brand was no longer available.[51]

In recent years the number of defectors has about equaled the number of new converts. But the total number of supermarkets has continued to increase, while the number using stamps has held constant, resulting in a smaller market share. In the vanguard of the exodus were companies that had waited until the established brands were no longer available and whose misgivings about stamps became self-confirming. Lawrence W. Bell, publisher of *Premium Practice,* has called them the "lifo merchants: last in, first out."

When managements predict to their stockholders that the transition from stamps will start with profit-encroaching temporary price cuts and lead to an improvement over pre-defection profit,[52] they conceptualize some combination of a downward shift in marginal cost and a downward movement along an initially elastic demand curve that eventually will become less elastic so that normal prices can be restored with impunity. This translation of management's intuition has the following implications.

If the stamp was ineffectual, the defector will be better off without it, at any volume. If the gift was functional, the short-term analysis may still be correct. The revenue curve of the user may be unresponsive near the market-price level but reveal a high elasticity when the operator is "buying volume" below full costs (including normal profit).

The retaliation from rivals when the prices are cut and when they are restored plus consumer responsiveness will determine the new equilibrium. If customers are very price-conscious it is a setting for cut-throat competition coupled with ease and noneconomic attractions of entry. And, at volumes below the level at which stamps were abandoned, the post-stamp marginal costs will not be parallel with pre-stamp nor even necessarily below them.

The alternative to market discipline is market chaos. Under perfect competition, price is the disciplinarian. But *"retail competition con-*

sists chiefly in varying services rather than varying prices." [53] The model imputed to management, above, breaks down when long-term stability is posited without some arbiter which possesses the economic characteristics of the effective stamp. Such a substitute, when found, will not be costless. An obvious alternative is government regulation of retailing but its implications will not be explored in this book. Thus the conclusion emerges that in a mixed economy with a fragmented retailing structure, methods of creating differentiation, such as the stamp, are needed for workable competition.

Summary of Stamp Sequence. By placing into an idealized framework some of the complex business conditions that form a backdrop for stamp adoption, retention, vacillation, and defection, the foregoing discussion may have conveyed a misleading idea of a smooth progression of events. But in fact the notion of a stamp sequence is like the product life cycle — a series of related changes whose course is neither inevitable nor regular. Nor does the stamp perform the same function in every store. Like the stages of the product life cycle, the process of stimulation — stabilization — saturation — separation typifies an aparent underlying pattern which may serve as an analytical frame of reference.

At the store level, stamp policy is a series of decisions which can be summarized in a simplified manner. See Figure 2. When an issuer offers a stamp, the retailer decides either to abstain or adopt. If he subscribes, the user must evaluate whether or not the stamp is advantageous for him. An ineffective stamp will be cancelled. If it is effective, competitors will retaliate in various ways, market conditions will change . . . Meantime the retailer continues the program but frequent re-evaluations are necessary.

As long as the pulling power of the stamp is virtually unimpaired, the retailer is at Stage 1 of the cycle. At Stage 2, extra growth due to the stamp has stopped, but it does confer many advantages upon the user. These advantages erode in Stage 3. If the medium is unproductive, the retailer proceeds to Stage 4. However the situation works itself out in a specific case, the fact remains that many supermarkets found the trading stamp serviceable; its acceptance has been widespread but never universal. The decision is not a zero-sum game in terms of aggregate profits and perhaps not even in volume. It may be noted that an extrapolation of the Wheel of Retailing which, historically, has had wide but not total applicability,[54] points to discount food operations as a plausible candidate for trading stamps.

Figure 2

STORE POLICY DECISIONS ON TRADING STAMPS

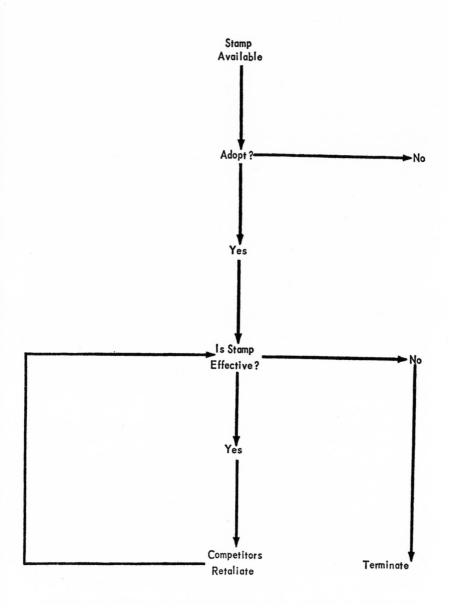

That could start a new sequence from overstoring (an excess of stores) to overstamping.

The reasons for stamp insistence and its repercussions may be analyzed but economic theory cannot predict the course of consumer preferences. In the dynamics of marketing there is no lasting formula to success. The reactions of consumers must be anticipated, perhaps even before they know what they will do. In a free economy, this is a risk of the entrepreneur.

ABSTENTION FROM STAMPS

Finally, it should be noted, a minority of supermarkets stayed clear of the entire sequence. As long as a store's practical capacity is absorbed and the retailer can hold his volume without stamps there is little reason why he should adopt them. Outlets that achieve distinctiveness by virtue of an isolated location (away from competition) or by some other means do not need them. A stamp is usually not functional in an unstable community with a heavy turnover of transients or tourists. In some areas, stamps are forbidden.

In a country as big as the United States, even a small fraction of consumers constitute a huge market. Just as a stamp will divert traffic to its users, some shoppers will select a store precisely because it does not give stamps. Consumers vary also in their susceptibility to price appeals; stamps may disturb the monolithic low-price image of a supermarket that has a successful history of cultivating economic shoppers. If the discounter's competitors which employ a strategy based on service remain successful, they will allow a price differential to continue. "Nonprice differentiation, based on pseudo as well as genuine factors, opens up a protected niche for the seller who stresses price." [55] The price-bargain and the service-bargain stores co-exist, each satisfying a different consumer segment. Virtually every grocery chain operates on a split basis: some units with stamps and some without. This flexibility underscores the diversities in the market and illustrates the retailer's striving to accommodate them.

And, in retrospect, it can be said that some managers should have climbed on the bandwagon when it got rolling. Thus there are many reasons why some supermarkets never used trading stamps. No single principle of use or abstention can encompass all the complexities of stamps at the supermarkets. The range of possibilities is extended even further when retailers other than supermarkets are considered.

CHAPTER V

SUPPLY THROUGH OTHER RETAILERS

Although the largest, supermarkets are not the only group of retailers that employ trading stamps. Indeed, as has been noted, the grocery store's stamp owes some of its effectiveness to other types of retail establishments in its trading area that disburse the same brand and *vice versa*. The motivations for stamp-giving by other trades usually are the same as the grocer's. But there are also differences, some of which will be discussed below.

Gasoline Stations. The major economic difference between the supermarket and the gasoline station is easily summarized: the latter's competitive situation is more atomistic. Entry is easier, the number of stations greater, the supplier's power stronger, the consumer's access to competitors simpler, the average transaction smaller, the wherewithal lower, and the stock of trade is more homogeneous. Price wars are a frequent occurrence.

No such phenomenon as the Wheel of Retailing has come to pass in the gasoline-station industry. From its start the industry has employed an operating efficiency which half a century later is still being imitated and adapted to other forms of retailing: drive-in service. But the gasoline-station industry has spun its wheels. Over the decades, neither the product offerings nor the convenience services have been changed materially so that the gasoline dealer has not kept pace with new developments in retailing and consumer behavior. Perhaps the most important omission — the most glaring contrast with food stores—has been the gasoline-station industry's prevention of self-service.

The industry's situation has not been helped by the multitude of service stations. During the Great Depression the number of gasoline retailers doubled. Since then it has remained below its prewar peak but the turnover among dealer-operated stations (owned or leased by supplying companies) is 25% annually. Among the stations pumping less than 100,000 gallons per year the annual turnover is 40%.[1] The station operator's level of compensation is very low, and ease of entry tends to keep it low. "In this sense the business is still overcrowded."[2]

"Many operators believe that they can handle a 40% increase in gasoline sales with no major change in physical facilities."[3] Under the circumstances a trading stamp adopted by a local supermarket can be very important, and there usually is a rush by neighboring gas stations to adopt the same brand for pump-priming, so long as franchises are available. About one-third of all United States gasoline service stations disburse stamps.

As far as these gummed tokens are concerned, many of the differences between supermarkets and gasoline stations are in degree stemming from their relative economic situations. The gasoline station proprietor pays more per stamp (smaller quantity), has a higher break-even point (steeper variable costs), takes more time disbursing them (no specialized personnel), loses more (lack of protection against the elements and against theft), and hates them more (subjective view of business). Besides these differences in degree there are important differences in kind.

The service station handles a much more limited line of merchandise than supermarkets do. The relationship with suppliers is unlike the supermarket's dealings with its vendors. Typically, a service station is tied to a single brand of gas; rent is a function of volume. "In many sections of the country, dealers believe that they are under heavy pressure (from suppliers and jobbers) to take on stamps."[4] But the policies of the retailers' gasoline suppliers have varied. Some have taken a neutral stance. Others have counseled their dealers not to adopt stamps.[5] Dealers in New Jersey have testified that their suppliers absorbed at least part of the cost of stamps through a rent adjustment.[6]

Stamp usage predominates among outlets of advertised brands of gasoline. Unless subsidized, the stamp cost increases the variable-cost differential between the brand outlets and the independents. The cross-elasticity of demand among retail stations is high. The demand to the industry is quite inelastic but to the dealer it is highly elastic. "We can't pass on this cost of trading stamps to the consumer," testified the executive secretary of the New Jersey Gasoline Retailers Association plaintively, "we have to absorb it."[7]

Discrimination may aggravate the proprietor's problems; a policy of granting stamps only to customers who express a wish for them appears to embarrass and rankle savers.[8]

Many operators resist the full-line forcing policy of some stamp companies. The dealers realize that the same customer who demands stamps on gasoline may consider their equivalent cash value in a single large transaction. Paradoxically, the expense is easier to absorb on tires, batteries, accessories, and especially on car repair. It is interesting that even when the sale of a homogeneous convenience item is combined in one outlet with an assortment of shopping and specialty goods, the differential in stamp sales-leverage between these types of goods is manifest.

Because of the narrow product line, the stamp expansibility of demand for gasoline is easier to compute than for the offerings of supermarkets. At the time of the New Jersey hearings, Regular grade of gasoline cost the dealers 23.9 cents per gallon and it sold at 28.9 cents.[9] The stamps cost about $125 per 50,000.[10] If the dealer gave 1 stamp per 10-cent sale (breakage disregarded) to every motorist, he increased his cost 3%. Some service station proprietors testified that due to their abstention from trading stamps, gasoline volume was down one-half or more from normal;[11] with stamps, volume rose 80% or more.[12] Defining expansibility of demand as the relative change in volume induced by a relative change in cost, with selling prices and other variables unchanged, one can compute it from these data as

$$\frac{-\,50\%}{-\,3\%} = 17, \text{ contraction due to lack of stamps and}$$

$$\frac{+\,80\%}{+\,3\%} = 27, \text{ expansibility due to adoption of stamps.}$$

These dealers' experiences were probably atypical but some schedules were filed with the state's Assembly Committee to "indicate the effect on gallonage when stamps are dropped and picked up. The purpose is to supply the evidence of the impact of stamps on our gasoline market."[13] These schedules all showed similar patterns. The most informative history was contributed by a dealer, in partnership with his father. The gasoline station's record revealed their experience as user, defector, and reinstator of trading stamps. The partners had been giving stamps until about August 15, 1962, when they "joined the movement"[14] and gave up stamps. Sales had been up 13% over the previous year in the seven months before the firm's separation from stamps. Thereupon the upward trend reversed sharply; in the first full month without stamps volume was 14% behind the previous year. By the end of October, the partners reverted to stamps; gallonage rose promptly and from December onward resumed the 13% rise. The monthly sales data put into the record follows.[15]

Pleading that the usage of stamps with gasoline be outlawed, the partner said that, in his opinion, the stimulation of business was not

Table 4

MONTHLY SALES RECORD OF A TEXACO GASOLINE STATION IN BRICK TOWNSHIP, NEW JERSEY (GALLONS)

MONTH	1961	1962	1963
January	29,762	32,885	36,409
February	25,328	30,778	34,467
March	32,022	35,445	41,200
April	31,882	35,298	
May	32,093	37,269	
June	35,731	42,398	
July	45,327	49,212	
August	42,299	41,856 ◄—Dropped Stamps	
September	37,927	32,616	
October	35,854	32,458 ◄—Reinstated Stamps	
November	36,759	38,089	
December	37,426	42,625	

SOURCE: New Jersey State Assembly. Public Hearing before Special Assembly Committee for Study of Trading Stamps and Similar Merchandising Devices, April 5, 1963, p. 51-A.

due to trading stamps. But on the basis of his action and his record, if one interprets that without stamps his sales were 86% of the previous year's and with stamps, 113 — an increase of 31% — the stamp expansibility of demand appears to have been about + 10.

More important than any particular computation, the testimony at the Hearing demonstrates that many dealers resent the high sales leverage of stamps as a personal insult as well as a threat. Gasoline retailers have often organized boycotts against trading stamps but these collusions may be illegal and have usually been short-lived. Hence the dealers seek special protective laws. The focus on a single product, the franchise system of selling advertised gasoline, and the political appeal of small business make attempted state regulation prohibiting incentives more likely in the gasoline station industry than in the supermarket field. But any protection from stamps is likely to be illusive, even if the laws are not struck down by the courts.

Regulations of conduct seem futile unless they are coupled with regulations of structure. As Stigler points out, the permanent gains or losses from government policy usually accrue to the owners of specialized resources.[16] If the petroleum industry allowed the dealer wider margins, they would attract more operators. This may accord with the interest of some refiners because they want more outlets for their gasoline. Indeed, the dealer-location policies of some refiner marketers may be partly responsible for the high incidence of failure at the retail level, avers Dirlam.[17] Since there is no evidence that consumers would prefer to pay a higher price for the convenience of having more stations, a special inducement to expand the number would seem to be a waste, both from the dealer's and the economy's points of vantage. "Gasoline could be sold on a lower margin if there were fewer stations in operation to share the existing volume . . ."[18] On the one hand, dealers clamor for enforced price floors. On the other hand, within three years after "Fair Trade" was instituted in New Jersey, the number of independent stations increased from 165 to 600.[19] The dealers' own testimony on the effect of stamps and the excessive competition in the industry seem to argue for a reduction in stations. The stamp may have acted as a mild rationalizer, discouraging some entry, but it has not been effective enough.

Several conclusions emerge from this brief portrayal and from due allowance for the intensified effect of corresponding elements noted in the last chapter's supermarket analysis. Trading stamps are to the service station what free maps, credit cards, and advertising are to the petroleum-marketers. Gasoline service stations in the aggregate have probably enjoyed no expansion in sales due to stamps. But the gummed tokens may temper some women's misgivings toward gasoline stations. If station operators cultivated volume on nongasoline as supermarket managers have on nonfood, stamps could be more profitable.

Other Retailers. Slightly less than 20% of trading stamps are disbursed in dry cleaning establishments; drug stores; camera shops; residential fuel firms; hardware, lumber supply, and paint stores; jewelry stores; department and variety stores; auto accessories stores; feed and farm suppliers; sporting goods; car dealers; and other outlets. They are the traditional base of the stamp system. In the late 1950's and in the 1960's between one-fifth and one-sixth of all dry cleaners and drug stores have been giving stamps; in the other retail sectors probably less than one-tenth of the stores have been participating. For those stores with homogeneous products the uses and effects of trading stamps are basically those that were discussed in the sections on supermarkets and gasoline stations. Obviously, some of the users have various means of differentiation including a diversified stock of goods and personal service. But the big difference is that food and gas are purchased frequently whereas customers visit stores offering other goods only occasionally. Hence savers do not become accustomed to these stores. There are some additional economic considerations which affect these remaining types of stamp-using retailers.

The heavy incidence of stamps among drug stores is somewhat surprising in view of that field's overall stability and profitability. It is conjectured that stamps may be a defensive mechanism against the sales shift of proprietary medicines and beauty aids and similar merchandise (not prescription drugs) to supermarkets and discount houses.

The gummed token has also been drawn into the expense-account economy. Some sellers of services to individuals and executives, such as restaurants and car rental agencies, can use stamps as an alternative to other forms of inducements brandished for selective patronage. These fields may be the scene of future increases in stamp use.

Among independent retailers, communitywide actions are consistent with joint profit maximization. Thus the exclusion of stamps or adoption of a single brand by all members of a shopping center represents an effort to integrate a locality's sales promotion policy. A boycott by say, all the gasoline dealers in a region has the same implication. The use of different brands of stamps within a community or within a line of retailing — along with abstentions by some firms — is consistent with independent or "monopolistically competitive" profit maximization.

What about the traditional stamp users? A small, high-margin store may find the service effective precisely because few other small retailers in its line use it. Advertising may be too speculative and too ineffectual, particularly if the store has no real bargains or unusual selections for sale. The gift may stimulate an expansion in volume important to the establishment but negligible from a market perspective. It may encourage cash sales or speed collections. The stamp also serves as a tangible token of appreciation, helping to cement the personal relationship between the proprietor and his trade. In addition, some department stores serve as redemption centers for their stamp brand and thereby receive the benefit of extra traffic through the rest of the store.

But compared to the large user, the small merchant has two major disadvantages. The issuers of the most popular brands solicit the best prospects first, so that only weak brands may be available to the small retailers. Most issuers have a volume-discount price structure; hence the small user pays the highest price.

Furthermore, the typical general-merchandise retailer views the system as a competitor whose line of premiums is a substitute for his own stock of trade. The implications of trade statistics on the redemption patterns of those separate listings which are part of a set (as a table and chairs) and of surveys by manufacturers,[20] however, favor a conclusion that much redemption merchandise is complementary to cash-market goods and that the stamp industry's 100 million catalogs incidentally stimulate dollar demand for the types of goods listed. More important, in spite of the external economies that the stamp has recently been offering, the fact that it did not penetrate more deeply into the miscellaneous types of traditional users seems to reflect its continued unsuitability for many of them.

Conclusions. The Wheel of Retailing brought supermarkets and other merchants many problems but also a productive opportunity in the form of trading stamps. Many a merchant realized that a commitment to stamp usage might in part preclude other promotions. Also, reliance on this service made some proprietors feel they had lost a degree of independence. The executives of most supermarket chains resisted what they hoped would be a fad. Many businessmen, however, also recognized that they could not disregard consumer wishes.

It turns out that even where a low-price policy exists as a consumer's alternative to stamps, price elasticity of demand often is much lower than promotional expansibility and, furthermore, the benefits from a stamp-usage policy are more durable. In general, the earlier the adoption, the bigger the organization, and the better the retailer's primary service, the more successful is his exploitation of this shopper magnet. In the supermarket industry the penetration became so deep that by the early 1960's some of the advantages had eroded and there have been quite a few disaffiliations. It would not be unexpected if stamp use tends to stabilize at somewhat lower levels than had been reached.

Most issuers protect their supermarket customers through exclusive franchises within their selling area. But policies on associate accounts vary. The practice of proximity selling (making the same brand available to nearby competitors)[21] nullifies the distinctiveness that a stamp can confer on its user. Such proliferation does not mean that the gift is ineffective. As long as shoppers want the bounty, their ability to withdraw patronage forces the subscribers to continue the service. Only when many consumers tire of the system or when other appeals are more powerful will retailers choose to abandon stamps — and encounter a new set of problems.

Chapter VI

THE STRUCTURE OF THE STAMP INDUSTRY

The coordinators of trading-stamp demand and supply are called the issuers in this work; here the focus is on them. The present chapter is concerned with the industry's structure; the following chapter with certain forces affecting this structure.

AN HISTORICAL NOTE

Generally, in the United States the trading stamp has been in heavy use when: (1) a business sector dealing frequently with consumers needed trading stamps as a gift; and (2) the consumer could accumulate enough stamps to make saving them worth while.

In the absence of either pre-condition, they have had but minor acceptance. They are not serviceable during rapid inflation when they lack the first-mentioned requirement. If pecuniary demand absorbs the total production capacity there is no need for either a sales stimulant or a collection catalyst. They are not strong during deep depression when they lack the second-mentioned requirement. If pecuniary purchasing power is inadequate for necessities there is no confidence in one's ability to complete such a program. At all stages of the business cycle, trading stamps have been vulnerable to legal prohibitions and harassments — both in this country and abroad. On the basis of these considerations it is possible to divide the 75-year history of American stamps into three periods: 1892-1915, 1916-1950, and 1951 to present.

Rapid growth took place between 1892 and 1915. As a payment and patronage incentive, trading stamps were used by department stores, mail-order houses, and many kinds of small-sized stores including grocery chains. Manufacturers of consumer goods furnished coupons exchangeable for trading stamps. Many booklets required only 990 stamps, and premiums were available for as few as 25.

A precipitous decline in 1916 was followed by three decades of stamp weakness. In the United States the setting for a stamp industry crash was inflation in the wake of Europe's World War I plus adverse legal enactments and decisions. Next, America entered the war; postwar there was first another round of inflation and then a brief but sharp depression. A crisis in the department-store trade was followed by a curtailment of promotions such as trading stamps. Department-store sales decreased, and the firms were saddled with heavy fixed costs from overbuilding before World War I. Grocery chains discontinued stamps as they converted their units into economy stores. Thus after 1916 the use of trading stamps was confined mainly to various small retailers as (1) a cash-payment incentive and (2) a feeble retaliatory medium against aggressive chains and bigger stores. Usage continued low during the prosperity of the 1920's; thereafter it almost collapsed. At the depth of the Great Depression the entire stamp industry's volume probably was less than The Sperry and Hutchinson Company's annual sales had been some three decades earlier. A slow recovery started after the mid-1930's and continued through the 1940's.

By mid-century, stamp usage was spreading rapidly, mainly among small food stores. The Sperry and Hutchinson Company serviced more than one-half of the market. The stamp's potency in independent stores led some larger retailers to consider the suitability of this promotional tool for their own organizations, but the strongest brand was not always available. S & H protects its accounts in their immediate selling area by not selling Green Stamps to their direct competitors. Since S & H refused to sever established relationships for the purpose of contracting with large organizations, by the mid-1950's some important supermarket chains established joint ventures or subsidiaries in order to control brands of their own. Most food executives were reluctant to adopt stamps, as noted in Chapter IV, but the public clamored for them. The stamp industry's volume grew rapidly until the early 1960's when America's largest supermarket chain adopted a newly established, independent stamp brand. During the 1960's S & H has held about 38% of the market. As the 1960's were drawing to a close, the supermarket's relative share of total stamp usage declined and the industry's volume plateau was increasingly sustained by different types of outlets and activities.

The above time spans chronicle the alternating fortunes of the stamp industry. Of course, the dates are necessarily arbitrary and the skeleton spare — at the sacrifice of much fascinating detail. Over the decades there has been surprisingly little change in the operating methods, the indictments, and the justifications of this controversial instrument. The earliest available documents about trading stamps sound unbelievably modern. Here appear to be the ingredients for a separate historical study. With the above background of the industry in mind, this discussion will take a static approach, mid-1960's, utilizing the latest available data.

GROWTH IN THE 1950's; MATURITY IN THE 1960's

Trading stamp establishments, as defined in the Census of Business, are those "primarily engaged in selling trading stamps to merchants, and redeeming such stamps with merchandise." The Standard Industrial Classification code of the issuers is 7396. Substitutes such as stamps for cash redemption, tape register plans, or advertising are excluded from this study because they differ, in concept and effect, from trading stamps for merchandise redemption.

In 1963, the United States Census of Business reports, the receipts of the stamp industry were $761,709,000—twice the amount shown for 1958. The stamp issuers maintained 923 administrative and sales offices plus 1835 redemption centers with total employment (at a date in March or November) of 16,721 persons and an annual payroll of $68,211,000 (preliminary data).[1] Department of Commerce data show that in 1958 there were 199 companies in this industry compared with 212 in 1963.

In terms of aggregates such as gross national product or total employment, the trading-stamp activity is tiny. For example, the reported industry employment is less than one-quarter of one-tenth per cent of total United States employment. Nevertheless, the trading stamp does exert substantial influence in the consumer sector; in certain retail sectors such as food, gasoline, dry cleaning services, and drug stores; and in selected manufacturing and services industries where the trading stamp's serviceability led to a concentration of its supply or demand. Similarly, its impact can be very heavy on a local basis.

As noted in a previous chapter, conditions in the supermarket industry around the early 1950's caused it to enlist the stamp's incentive function. There followed a sudden spurt in stamp volume, with sales doubling every two years. In the one year 1955 to 1956 sales of stamps again doubled and then paused on this plateau for two years. After 1958, stamp volume rose at a slower rate, about 10 to 20% annually, until it reached a new plateau in the mid-1960's. Since then stamp volume has been rising no faster than retail sales. Table 5 presents a summary of stamp industry growth since 1955.

Throughout a year, the issue of stamps is fairly even. From month to month the demand for food is level and the seasons of other users are offsetting. The call on premiums, on the other hand, is tied to

Table 5

ESTIMATES OF TRADING STAMP INDUSTRY GROWTH
1955 - 1966

Year	Trading Stamps Issued (Billions)	Number Stamps Redeemed (Billions)	Average Price Per 1000 Stamps	Total Retail Sales (Billions) (1)	% Retail Sales by Stamp Users	Total Retail Grocery Sales (Billions) (2)	% Grocery Sales by Stamp Users
1955	82	61.7	$2.29	$183.851	5%	$36.919	11%
1956	168	121.3	2.20	189.729	10	39.180	23
1957	180	150.8	2.16	200.002	10	42.444	30
1958	192	163.6	2.12	205.353	10	44.547	31
1959	210	178.3	2.09	215.413	11	46.043	34
1960	255	228.0	2.07	219.529	14	48.339	38
1961	300	259.5	2.05	218.811	16	49.910	42
1962	350	298.0	2.03	235.351	17	52.124	47
1963	364	328.0	2.02	246.312	17	53.527	46
1964	377	339.0	2.00	261.630	17	57.272	46
1965	389	350.0	2.00	283.950	16	61.068	44
1966 Prel.	397	360.5	2.00	304.961	15	65.098	42

(1) Sources: Statistical Abstracts, 1955 to 1959; Monthly Retail Trade Reports for 1960-1966.
(2) Sources: Department of Commerce; Monthly Retail Trade Reports.
Information supplied by S&H Corporate Research Department.

holidays, and some 20% of annual redemptions occur during the Christmas season. Thus in its relations with both users and savers, the issuer is largely responsive rather than initiating.

As a supplier of stamps and premiums, an issuer contracts directly with numerous small users and operates redemption centers for savers on a local basis. The stamp issuer also deals with the headquarters of large users in each region, under conditions of bilateral oligopoly. As a buyer of premiums and services, a trading-stamp company enlists vendors in national or even international markets and employs factors of production wherever it operates.

ECONOMIC FUNCTIONS

The many places where the trading stamp impinges on the economy can be grouped loosely under three different economic functions. A multiplier function operating for the benefit of the general economy describes the influence of stamps on other businesses — the creation of additional business activity. An incentive function, for the user's benefit, aims to rationalize retailing; i.e., to have an efficient number of stores. A retailer function assists the consumer in increasing his scale of living by maximizing the delivery of premiums. Of course, these functions are not so discrete as an outline of them suggests. The incentive and the retailer functions, particularly, tend to overlap or clash. Hence they are suboptimized.

Multiplier Function. The activities of the stamp company in the retail market, it is often pointed out, stimulate other segments of the economy.[7] Although impressive, the evidence that much of the merchandise moved via the stamp channel represents a net boost to business activity is indirect and will not be developed here.

Incentive Function. In their present application at the retail level, trading stamps function primarily as a differentiation device. However deplored by some capitalistic and communistic philosophers, differentiation for patronage inducement has a long history which includes branding, advertising, premiums, and samples. Because differentiation can deliver many utilities that transcend ideology, these promotional methods have been employed in mercantilistic Europe, in capitalistic America, and in communistic Russia.

Another function for retailers, usually stressed by industry spokesmen, is that the trading stamp fosters efficiency among its users. The idea is to reduce the frictions of the process of fitting heterogeneous supply to heterogeneous demand. An effective stamp helps expand

and regularize patronage which brings internal economies to the user. By building groups of complementary users, the issuer provides an external economy for all of them, and by operating a redemption center, it paves the way for their customers' choice from a broader stock than any single type of user could provide.

Retailer Function. The trading stamp company also helps to enrich the consumer's scale of living. This view of the stamp, which is examined in later chapters, focuses on its similarity to mail-order firms (i.e., catalog), retail chains (i.e., redemption centers), discount houses (skim merchandising), which, too, have overcome the opposition of established channels because of consumer support. "Actually," said Professor H. L. Grathwohl, "the stamp company might be considered as a new form of retailer."[3] In organizing a firm, the stamp-issuing entrepreneur assumes the economic function of risk-taking. Preparing a catalog entails the economic function of value determination; publishing it, the stamp company supplies information utility. During the catalog's validity period the company maintains a stock of the listed premiums, thus providing time utility. Their availability at redemption centers furnishes place utility; the act of redemption yields possession utility.

The stamp is a medium for reducing inertia in the acquisition of wanted merchandise. An effective stamp helps expand and proportion consumption in ways that increase the citizens' satisfaction. By reducing the perceived sacrifice, the issuer helps close the gap between the consumer's standard and scale of living; by arranging the flow of goods more efficiently than conventional retailers, it delivers real savings. It is an axiom in economics that in time all goods and services will have substitutes. Proximity selling of stamps (providing competitors with the same brand), games and contests, discount prices, and many other tactics may, in the long run, weaken the stamp's ability to make or keep retailing more efficient than it would be without stamps. In the future, the economic justification for the gummed coupon may hinge increasingly on its ability to provide wanted merchandise more efficiently than conventional channels.

Conflicting Objectives. The incentive and the retailer functions cannot be maximized simultaneously. In fact, they may work at cross-purposes. Differentiation through stamp plans may be conducive to efficiency in retailing. A small number of plans tends to concentrate patronage among the optimum number of retailers. On the other hand, the blanketing of a single brand enables savers to fill their books faster, thus increasing the delivery of premiums, but it forgoes rationalization. Whether consumers would prefer stamps primarily for rationalization of stores or for receipt of premiums is a moot point.

Among the stamp companies, distribution policies vary depending on whether the issuer's interests in his brand are primarily short-term or long-term. If the stamp is viewed as a profitable sideline or a temporary opportunity, the issuer may try for quick profits by maximizing the sale of as many stamps to as many retailers as possible. Provided all the associate accounts handle goods that are independent or complementary to the key account, the latter obtains greater external economy as the proliferation of stamps becomes deeper and wider. Similarly, most savers want as many stamps from as many places as possible. But there are also sound reasons why some firms do not espouse such a utopian policy.

Some issuers, for example, oppose the giving of excess stamps. Varying rates of disbursement can impair a stamp company's goodwill with both savers and users. The public would not know what to expect when it responds to the sign, "We give XYZ-Brand Stamps." Inconsistent policies engender dissatisfaction of customers when a lower rate is given than on the previous purchase. Some retailers, however, can afford double or triple stamping which will attract shoppers from another retailer's franchise area. Frustration of the protection intent could ignite an intra-brand war and weaken the issuer's customers. And if the users' rate of disbursement varies, the issuer cannot guarantee a ceiling on their stamp cost. Besides these possible problems within a given brand, excess disbursement can also cause dislocations of a more general nature.

The issuer oriented toward continuity of his brand is likely (a) to prefer a fixed rate of disbursements and (b) to protect a territorial franchise. Both these policies can be analyzed in terms of decreasing returns. At the intensive margin, a large block of bonus stamps on a particular article defrayed by the user is unlikely to recoup his usual profit even if the quantity sold doubles. Moreover, the "extra" sales may be substitutions for revenue that the same user would have realized at the time on other goods or at a later date when the customer would normally replenish his needs. Finally, an escalation of stamp ratios can set off ratios-retaliation by rivals with other brands. None of these possibilities is in accord with the user's long-run interests. Any such disadvantage to the user concerns the issuer as well. A seller-buyer relationship can endure only if it is mutually profitable.

At the extensive margin, the issuer keeps enlisting poorer and poorer accounts and the pioneer-user loses his distinctiveness. Thus a fixed-ratio and a protected-franchise policy accord with a fundamental goal of stamp-brand continuity.

The shared interest of issuers and savers in saturation of retail channels with stamps is expedient but such a distribution policy deprives the user of an expense-offsetting differentiation. Were the gift used mainly as a cash payment incentive, it would be more effective with intensive than with selective distribution. If this analysis is correct, it implies that in the 1920's and 1930's a franchise policy on discount stamps, as they were then called, may have been detrimental to the three parties; the issuers, the users, and the savers. But when the main purpose of the boon is enterprise differentiation — as in the 1950's and 1960's — the need for franchising is manifest.

ORGANIZATION

The trading stamp industry's volume is divided about 2:1 between companies which are independent issuers and those that are users' cooperatives. The first type is exemplified by The Sperry and Hutchinson Company, Gold Bond Stamp Company, E. F. MacDonald Stamp Company, and King Korn Stamp Company, whose customers almost exclusively are separate businesses. The second type includes such joint ventures as Top Value Enterprises, Inc. and Blue Chip Stamp Company plus subsidiaries of supermarket chains, e.g., Merchants Green Trading Stamp Company and Triple-S Trading Stamp Company — all of which were organized by users but sell also to non-owners. The private stamp company, a retailer with an individual plan, is so insignificant that it can be omitted from this discussion. Until 1966 all stamp firms were closely-held corporations. Many are subsidiaries of large public companies. In 1966 a secondary offering made some stock in the industry's leader available to the public; now The Sperry and Hutchinson Company is listed on the New York Stock Exchange. In view of estate tax laws and financial opportunities plus the advantages of investor support, perhaps other companies will follow.

Independent Companies. The independent stamp company operates like any other retailer — at arm's length from its customers and its suppliers. Its goal is its own long term prosperity. The independent issuer is a specialist who promotes and supplies his brand for continuous acceptance. The economics of "to make" versus "to buy" — which apply to the considerations of user-issuer versus independent issuer — have been treated in other books at length and will not be repeated in this analysis. It is of interest, however, to point out the salient characteristics and distinctions of the user-owned operations.

User-Owned Companies. Most of the currently prominent firms of this type were organized as a defensive or retaliatory measure against the independents after the latest wave of popularity in the 1950's. In the users' joint venture the primary interest of most owners is their retail organization, and conflicting attitudes toward stamps are reported frequently. The owners of Blue Chip Stamp Company, accused by the Justice Department of first conspiring to suppress the use of trading stamps and then jointly establishing the company in an attempt to create a monopoly, have been at odds for some time. After several of the principals contested various proposals for settlement of the suit, the United States District Court at Los Angeles approved a consent judgment in 1967. Under its terms the owners must sell at least 55% of the company's stock, and the Company must sell at least one-third of its assets.[4] One of the owners of Top Value Enterprises, Inc., the Stop and Shop chain of supermarkets, discontinued its stamp in 1965. Another minority stockholder, Allied Super Markets, Inc., sued Top Value in 1966, charging that it gave preferential treatment to its major shareowner.[5]

Nevertheless, the users' cooperative has certain inherent advantages over the independent company. The most important superiority is a core of outlets which creates demand through the brand's exposure to shoppers and facilitates supply through the reduction in selling expense. Sales of the captive brands to nonowners generate cash and profits for the stamp-issuing retailer. A user running his own stamp company can tailor its policies to his particular benefit and he may be able to lessen the managerial, physical, and financial duplications that two separate enterprises would ordinarily necessitate. For example, the Merchants Green Trading Stamp Company, a subsidiary of Food Fair Stores, Inc., is run by a long-time employee of the parent organization. In addition to its separate redemption centers, Merchants Green displays samples at service counters in some Food Fair stores, maintains offices in the Food Fair Building, and shares warehouse space with the parent. The owner has a net worth of about $100 million. The Dun & Bradstreet report on Merchants Green Trading

Stamp Company includes the following summary: "This corporation is backed by a financially strong parent and functions for the benefit of its parent."[6] At May 1, 1965, the stamp company's total stock was 200 shares at $100 par value ($20,000); Retained Earnings were $2,613,234; its Cash was $50,300; and its Total Liabilities, $8,225,777.[7]

In contrast, an independent stamp company ordinarily needs a different financial structure. For example, Holden Trading Stamp Co. whose sales are perhaps one-third the sales of Merchants Green reported an owners equity almost as large. At January 30, 1965, Holden had 500,000 shares at $1 per ($500,000) outstanding and Surplus was $1,826,018. This independent company also reported Cash of $315,220 and Total Liabilities of $5,070,632.[8] In this example of two companies with almost equal owners equities, the captive firm could, with one-sixth the cash balance of the independent corporation, support sales about three times as high and carry debts about 1.6 times as high. Although the exact ratios differ from firm to firm, such a pattern appears to be typical. Thus the form of the organization influences the issuer's purpose, efficacy, and financing.

SIZE AND CONCENTRATION

Although retailing is a local activity and most retail lines are un-concentrated, in the trading-stamp industry the five largest firms service about 80% of the market. Of course, personal ability is necessary for a particular firm's eminence but external forces buffeting the industry are such that some few companies are likely to emerge with high market shares.

Structural Determinants of Size. Many aspects of the stamp system are conducive to oligopoly. Some of the impetus comes from the supply side. The stamp's heaviest disbursers are chain stores who can achieve managerial economies and augment marketing effectiveness by aligning their outlets' promotional efforts. Hence the chains will, in most cases, use the same brand in all stores where they give stamps. Such a uniformity is virtually assured when a chain has a brand of its own but it can also be achieved by using a widely known independent stamp brand. Even an independent issuer is likely to channel a large proportion of its tokens through large users. Much of the business is transacted under conditions of bilateral oligopoly. For example, Sperry and Hutchinson obtains about one-third of its service revenues from 12 licensees and the balance from about 55,000. Most other companies' sales are even more concentrated.

Another point favoring national or regional brands is that one-fifth of all stamps flow through gasoline stations. In this case each individual user is small and depends on wide complementary availability of his stamp brand for much of its effectiveness. The same expectations are held by other small users who hope to benefit from wide distribution of their stimulation device.

These pressures toward oligopoly are reinforced on the demand side. A name well known for financial strength and fair dealing inspires public confidence. Most savers collect only a single brand or two. Stamps are worth while only in large quantities; hence most markets can accommodate only a handful of brands. Their local popularity is based on association with one of the few stores in the area that makes frequently recurring sales to the same customers. Moreover, since Americans change their residences often, they prefer brands whose availability is wider than local. Before other aspects of the incentive function are examined, a few other impulsions to large size will be cited.

In its retailing function the large stamp company enjoys the economies of scale typical of the merchandising industry. For example, due to the law of large numbers a large volume of redemptions can be supported on a relatively smaller inventory base than a smaller volume. Quantity purchasing, carload shipping, and specialized facilities offer the usual cost advantages.

Administratively, a few key accounts entail smaller selling and servicing costs than thousands of small customers. And there is still another spur to large size in the trading-stamp business. The larger company is better able to absorb the expense entailed in preventing or countering the numerous legal harassments to which the industry is subjected. They include investigations, public hearings, statutes, regulations, and law suits on a national, state, and local basis. Thus it is not surprising that a handful of companies has emerged with a market share noticeably above the rest of the industry.

A size large enough to strengthen the likelihood of survival may be achieved with extensive or intensive coverage. Here the evidence on returns to scale is conflicting. A national company has many advantages. But the fact that only one company operates in as many as 47 states breeds a suspicion that some of its aggressive competitors may have encountered a point of diminishing returns.

One limitation on growth is protection of key accounts or franchises. Since the markets served by the various regional chains overlap, an exclusive arrangement to serve one organization may preclude the stamp issuer's market extension. Moreover, the "capture" of a

sizeable account typically involves a heavy capital outlay at high
risk. The new user might require special research programs to show
how stamps can be used most effectively. It may also want assistance
in preparing to use them. This aid may take the form of loans to
improve facilities or of additional redemption centers near or in
its stores.

A narrower operation can cultivate a segment of the population
whose tastes do not harmonize with the necessarily general orientation of the large company's catalog. The regional stamp firm can
specialize geographically, capitalizing on its area's differences from
the rest of the country. Although Americans change their address
frequently, most stay in the same general vicinity. In a 1966 survey,
only 6% of the respondents indicated that moving caused a problem
on their stamps. Thus a regional company can impart that personalized flavor — locally made goods for local consumption — that is
so important in merchandising. On the supply side, transportation
charges will be lower and replenishment faster. The more compact
the area of operation, the simpler is the coordination. Since the legal
atmosphere limits volume discounts, the smaller company is likely
to buy most articles at the same price as the larger. Apparently there
are some deterrents to the inherent tendency toward large-size firms
in the trading-stamp industry.

The economics of expansion were quantified as follows by an executive of a medium-size stamp firm. He estimated that he would need
a prospective retail volume base of about $15 million for six years
in order to finance a small new redemption center. His breakeven
calculation follows.

Table 6

ENTRY INTO A NEW AREA

Sales: 30,000 pads		$300,000
Merchandise cost	$202,000	
Redemption center exp.	22,000*	
Marketing expense	60,000**	
Administrative expense	16,000	300,000
Profit or Loss		— 0 —

*Includes $3,000 to be amortized in each of six years.
**Includes $25,000 special marketing campaign.

Statistics on Concentration and Size. "The trading stamp business
is concentrated in a few large companies. The 10 largest stamp companies accounted for about 70 per cent of all stamps that were sold

to retailers during 1956,"[9] stated the United States Department of Agriculture. In that year 33 companies with revenue above $1 million accounted for about 90% of the market. In the 11 years since that time the degree of concentration has increased markedly. According to a study published by the National Commission on Food Marketing, in the mid-1960's about 85 to 90% of the stamp business was shared by the ten largest firms, including Eagle Stamp Company.[10] Since most of these companies are regional, even this estimate understates the degree of local-market concentration. In one exceptional case, a company confining itself to one large state captured two-thirds of its market.[11] The stamp system's natural tendency toward high market share and the high likelihood of monopoly if franchise restrictions are absent are evidenced by that company's rapid penetration into some metropolitan markets within the state, which approached 90%.[12]

More specific evidence of companies' size and growth is available from Table 7 which presents the sales record of most large firms. The data were gathered mainly from government sources. The only major omission is Gold Bond Stamp Company, believed to rank approximately third in the industry. It may be noted that the four largest companies shown in the table (which excludes Gold Bond Stamp Company) accounted for 72% of the $761.7-million industry volume reported by the United States Census of Business for 1963. Based on Census statistics, the concentration estimate published by the National Commission on Food Marketing was probably too low. In general, then, specialization on the demand side and apparent economies of scales on the supply side plus institutional pressures foster high concentration in the stamp industry. This leads to the question whether it is an open or closed oligopoly.

EASE OF ENTRY

Traditionally, the retail sector has been characterized by ease of entry and difficulty of survival. As conditions in the retail sector change, opportunities for a service like trading stamps open and close: another line of trade in need of the incentive medium provides room for new stamp issuers; a defection squeezes the established firms. For example, in the middle 1950's many serious businessmen organized new stamp firms which achieved great success. Other ventures failed to achieve sufficient acceptance of their brands or discontinued operations after the loss of a key account.

As demonstrated by a company organized in 1961, the best way to enter is to start with a core of outlets that will give exposure to the

Table 7
TIME SERIES, ANNUAL SALES OF SELECTED TRADING STAMP COMPANIES
(THOUSAND DOLLARS)

YEAR ENDED: SOURCES: Year	December 31 (c) The Sperry and Hutchinson Company	March 31 subseq. (a) Top Value Enterprises, Inc.	June 30 current (b) Blue Chip Stamp Company	January 31 subseq. (a) E. F. MacDonald Stamp Company	July 31 current (a) King Kom Stamp Company
1956	138,104	45,771	5,306		Not Available
1957	160,430	58,918	8,372		Not Available
1958	177,126	65,164	10,001		Not Available
1959	203,970	79,727	30,665		6,645
1960	230,477	88,965	48,230		7,280
1961	268,465	94,506	56,685	Started in Late 1961	10,181
1962	296,501	104,745	(*)	64,919	13,565
1963	304,555	113,072	68,188	66,186	21,593
1964	322,296	118,299	71,739	63,427	23,546
1965	330,610	123,573	80,915	58,857	23,932

* Fiscal year changed to end of February.

NOTE: Due to differences in accounting methods the data are not strictly comparable.

SOURCES:
(a) Michigan Annual Report, various years, filed with the Michigan Corporation and Securities Commission, Lansing, Mich.
(b) Supermarket News, July 18, 1966
(c) The Sperry and Hutchinson Company, Preliminary Prospectus in the offering of Common Stock, April 20, 1966, pp. 4-5.

new brand and make the costs of entry worth while. In its first full year of operations, this independent issuer achieved a volume of $65 million. Within five years after it was formed, the company advertised that it outsold the industry's leader in "a surprising number of major metropolitan markets (including New York)." [13] Another outstanding sales success was a users' joint venture organized in 1955 which billed $20 million during the first eight months of its operations. Many other recent entrants into the industry established their brands at a slower pace, and they, too, are continuing to operate profitably.

Aside from the intensively cultivated fields (supermarkets and service stations), entry opportunties may exist among the many trades and services where the inroads of stamps have been negligible. Retailing trends often diverge; one subgroup moving toward austerity and another toward services. A chain of variety stores or discount houses that disdained stamps yesterday may tomorrow become a user that provides a core of redemption station, thus reducing the absolute-capital barrier to entry. Another type of entry opportunity may be based on service improvement. One such possibility was removed by some state governments when they enacted a cash-redemption option or requirement. If savers had really wanted cash redemption and established companies failed to provide that service, it could have been furnished by a newcomer. But many other features and terms of the stamp system remain available for a competitive thrust. As in many fields there are often more rewards for the successful innovator than the unimaginative imitator.

In the short run, the fact that in each area there is room for but a handful of stamp brands is a barrier to newcomers. It is reinforced by the importance of brand continuity. For example, among the twelve licensees that account for about one-third of S & H's revenues, eleven have subscribed to this brand for over 10 years and one for over 5 years. Unless a line of trade is saturated, however, existing franchises may constitute a pathway into a market. Like advertising agencies that do not accept competing clients, the stamp firm that awards local exclusivities virtually paves the way for others. Its users' competitors need an as yet uncommitted brand. If there seems to be no room for another brand, there are always the possibilities of buying out the owners of existing companies or of offering their customers a more attractive arrangement.

The merchandise plan of a company is an open book. Administrative and selling operations are well known and easily imitated. Operation of a stamp company seems to call for the integrity and acumen usually required in business plus special merchandising sense. There are obviously many challenges in such areas as selling, finance, materials management, and coordination, but these call for expertise and astuteness which, with varying emphases, are needed in every line. A stamp plan has no patent or technological secret.' If profits were really so fabulous as some opponents allege,[14] the owners of existing companies would be deluged with offers, and promoters of new brands would organize advertising campaigns, original approaches, or other ways of gaining a foothold.

In addition there is a feature peculiar to the system which invites entry: customers help finance the newcomer's operations. After a new firm has transferred its stamps for cash there is a distributed lag before they are presented for premiums. The initial redemption rate is very low but, soon, it jumps sharply. Even if the rate seems to settle after several years the tails of all previous redemption distributions continue to exert an upward push. Moreover, the current rate may be expected to fall when the company increases its issues substantially and, conversely, the redemption rate should rise in a year of sales decline. This pattern holds for successful companies generally. Even the work sheets of a small firm, filed with a government bureau, reflected this type of experience. But it is not a perfect demonstration, other variables also influence the results. The record is reproduced in Table 8.

It may be noted that in the company's first few years its redemption rates were negligible. But there was a build-up in the wake of the sales spurt of the early 1950's. By 1954 the current redemption rate had stabilized in the 90's and a comparison of sales and current redemption rates over the following decade shows that the direction of changes from the previous year were almost always inversely correlated. Sales rose and the redemption rate dropped (compared to the previous year) in 1955, 1957, 1959, 1963, and 1964. In 1956 and 1965 the upward push on the redemption rate from previous sales apparently swamped the negligible sales rises. Sales declined and, as expected, the current redemption rate rose in 1958 and 1962. The usual inverse correlation did not hold in 1960 and 1961. By the time the report was filed, the company's latest five-year moving average of redemptions had climbed to 96%.

The prospect of initial cash inflows has served to draw new entrants, sometimes with disastrous results. The ebullience of the 1950's attracted a few promoters, called "hotelroom operators" in the trade, who sold stamps but lacked a durable organization to redeem them.

Table 8
COMPUTATION OF ESTIMATED LIABILITY FOR COMPANY X STAMPS
OUTSTANDING AT MARCH 31, 1965

	Small Books Sold	Small Books Redeemed	Redemption Percent
Prior to 1949	46,000	34,300	74.57
1949	48,383	14,294	29.54
Jan. 1, 1950 to Mar. 31, 1950	31,696	11,548	36.43
Year Ended Mar, 31, 1951	164,458	110,580	67.24
1952	278,020	190,222	68.42
1953	352,241	298,251	84.67
1954	391,568	377,490	96.40
1955	427,882	389,788	91.10
1956	434,136	402,266	92.66
1957	507,115	460,009	90.71
1958	494,681	479,429	96.92
1959	564,954	516,300	91.39
1960	583,170	545,264	93.50
1961	645,045	604,298	93.66
1962	593,510	609,958	102.77
1963	608,860	585,432	96.15
1964	616,480	578,798	93.89
1965	620,118	589,661	95.08
	7,408,317	6,797,888	91.76
Five year Average			
Five years Ended 3/31/ 1961	2,794,965	2,605,300	93.21
1962	2,881,360	2,755,249	95.62
1963	2,995,539	2,861,252	95.51
1964	3,047,065	2,923,750	95.95
1965	3,084,013	2,968,147	96.24
Books sold thru Mar. 31, 1961	4,969,349		
Unredemption estimated @ 5%	248,467	4,720,882	
Books sold. yr. ended Mar. 31, 1962	593,510		
Mar. 31, 1963	608,860		
Mar. 31, 1964	616,480		
Mar. 31, 1965	620,118		
	2,438,968		
Unredemption estimated @ 4%	97,559	2,341,409	
		7,062,291	
Redemption thru Mar. 31, 1965		6,797,888	
Estimated Books to be Redeemed		264,406	
Estimated Liability (264,403 Books @ 1.63 each)	$430,976.89		

The deceit of these outsiders — and their wildcat predecessors half a century before — furnishes much of the "evidence" cited in attacks on the stamp system.

But it is also true that ease of entry into the business is sometimes exaggerated. "'On a 'crash' basis, a large stamp operation can be organized, installed, and launched in 5 days from the date of decision," a business consultant was quoted in a brief filed with the Securities and Exchange Commission.[15] This document was entered on behalf of an antistamp group in an unsuccessful petition to have trading stamps regulated as securities and have the companies prosecuted for failure to register their issues. Such actions against the industry have become a part of its structure and will be discussed next.

CHAPTER VII

COMPETITION IN THE STAMP INDUSTRY

The structure of the stamp industry and the individual companies within it have developed partly in response to the usual economic pressures. The structure reflects the needs of the consumers and retailers whom the industry serves. Among these forces are some pulling toward cooperation and many others pushing into rivalry.

LEGAL-LEGISLATIVE ATTACKS

Like most new forms of retailing, the stamp industry has been under sharp attack from various entrenched interests ever since its inception. Indeed, in its early history the stamp industry was sometimes prosecuted under Gift Enterprise laws which had been enacted to protect consumers from fraudulent terms of sale before stamps had been conceived. In most cases it was held that the law was inapplicable. Over the years, the onslaught has generally taken five additional forms: (1) Specific prohibition in whole or in part. (2) Prohibitive or discriminatory taxation. (3) Restrictive regulation. (4) Application of Fair Trade and other price maintenance laws. (5) Escheat of unredeemed stamps.

Whereas the early actions aimed at outright prohibition, in recent decades the tendency has been to introduce innocent-sounding proposals which would make the system unworkable. For example, a requirement that each stamp display prominently the true value of all premiums is conceptually defective since each premium has innumerable different prices which, further, are subject to change; compliance also is physically impossible because the fingernail-size piece of paper lacks the space to show much data legibly. Sometimes a spite law is enacted and wends its way through the judicial machinery before being declared unconstitutional or otherwise disposed of. "One could write a book about the laws and interpretations affecting the use of trading stamps,"[1] noted one economist. But instead of delving into the technicalities of jurisprudence, this study merely mentions the existence of various harassments. On the whole, the American people oppose very strongly the outlawing of trading stamps, and in nearly every case the courts ultimately decided in favor of freedom in the marketplace. It is mainly because of the pluralistic American system that trading stamps have survived seven decades of prosecution. The frequency of proceedings has had some effect on individual corporate structure, requiring, for example, specialized house counsel or suitably staffed legal departments. It is at once a force for external secrecy and for public-relations service. Strategies differ; some firms seem to be uncooperative, others are informative, and a few companies try both approaches, reflecting possibly internal differences of opinion.

Many of the actions against the industry have taken the form of joint proceedings against several companies. Although these attacks might have encouraged some measure of cooperative defense, most actions are defended unilaterally. Among the firms, competition is vigorous.

RIVALRY

The stamp industry's turbulent history, conflicting economic functions, organizational dichotomy, high penalty for shortcomings, and apparent ease of entry set the stage for active competition. On both the supply and demand sides, trading-stamp companies vie at every stage of the operating cycle. The rivalry is especially severe in the sale of enterprise differentiation to retailers because the exclusivity and continuity features of the system lead to a high probability that a contract will be a requirements arrangement that will last for a long time. Toward that end, each issuer contends for consumers' insistence on his brand. As buyers, trading-stamp companies strive for efficient deployment of factors, some of which need to be specialized and therefore may be in limited supply. Finally, the companies compete also in product-extension, market-extension, and other policy-level areas.

Competition for Users. "Competition among stamp companies is so keen that they use many inducements to capture a retailer's business."[2] Stamp companies prepare formal presentations for major prospects such as a food chain or a large independent department store. If the retailer seems especially desirable, the companies will outdo each other in trying to sign him. Prices are scaled according to the quantity of stamps used. Each company is eager to register a large outlet because its enlistment helps to recruit small noncompeting dealers in the same area. The smaller retailers are solicited by each stamp company's local salesman. According to sworn testimony, the proselyting of a competing stamp company's licensees is common practice. This was put on the record, for example, in 1962 when the Gold Bond Stamp Company sued the E. F. MacDonald Stamp Company. The plaintiff asked for an injunction against the defendant's urging users to break their contracts.

As noted, the smaller users pay a higher price per stamp than the large ones. This policy is one of several reasons why, in spite of vigorous competition, the average realization of all issuers is not identical. The spread is quite wide; the most expensive major brand costs 40% more, on average, than the lowest priced one. Stamp companies with revenues mainly from numerous small accounts may be expected to realize a higher average price and to incur higher marketing expenses than a company serving principally large users.

Another cause of the price difference lies in the organizational dichotomy, also discussed previously. In those cases where the issuer is owned by the user, the latter, of course, sets the price at which the service is "sold" to itself. This could be a matter of bookkeeping convenience. The wholly-owned issuer may be credited with a lower or higher price than the average; the internal arrangement need not coincide with the equilibrium that would result from arm's length bargaining between an independent stamp company and its customers.

The independent's price list is largely the resultant of its market information and judgment. The policy of the vertically integrated companies, however, may have an effect on the independent issuer. The latter must keep its customers competitive with their own rivals which use self-issued stamps. In addition, the independent firm would not like to encourage its large clients to start a system of their own. Finally, each stamp firm must contend with distant substitutes; enterprise differentiation might be attained through personalization of service, contests, aggressive pricing, and no stamps.

Perhaps the most important explanation of the price variation is the unlike effectiveness among brands. The value that they provide may not be the same from company to company. The retailer is paying for enterprise differentiation that increases his traffic and boosts his sales; a higher payment for a strong business magnet may be more efficient than a low price for a feeble one. In competing for a prospect's business, the stamp companies offer separate "products," depending on whether their policy is to award local exclusivities, protect accounts selectively, or sell without restriction. Which one of these services is most productive for the user depends on many variables; the point is that prices of competing brands are not directly comparable because of product differentiation and institutional peculiarities.

In addition, the contract provisions themselves are subject to competitive pressures. The issuers vie in payment terms, dealer supports, and termination clauses that they offer. The "sweeteners" may take the form of displays, signs, dispensing machines, etc. — either free or at a nominal charge. Some companies offer free or cooperative advertising. They may or may not leave to the user the decisions on which goods to disburse stamps and in what ratio. They may rent and operate redemption centers or order desks on the user's premises. After the account is signed, the issuer's salesman will strive to keep it satisfied by frequent visits during which he can advise his client and settle any problems. Since the issuer's customers have a derived demand, the relationship is likely to be an enduring one if the consumer insists on the brand. Hence all stamp firms contend for the public's allegiance.

Competition for Savers. At the consumer level, brand choice is almost as definitive as in the case of users. Whereas retailers ordinarily handle one brand exclusively, most savers keep track of no more than two. Savers also are loath to change brands. In sum, each stamp company faces similar pressures to enroll a consumer as it does to enroll a retailer. Hence it promotes its brand vigorously to the public and strives to deliver superior satisfactions to its savers.

Many a stamp executive is convinced that his firm offers the "best" premiums and is desirous to tell the public about his line. For most companies the catalog is probably the single largest consumer-promotion expense and much care is lavished upon it to make it stand out over the others. In the realm of mass communication, the companies employ all conventional advertising media. In 1961, The Sperry and Hutchinson Company reportedly spent $2¼ million — one-half in network television, one-quarter in magazines, and the balance in spot television and newspapers.[3] This was the year before "earnings from operations in 1962 and 1963 were adversely affected by increased expenditures for advertising required by competitive conditions . . ."[4] In the first half of 1962 E. F. MacDonald Stamp Company reportedly spent $2 million on spot television alone.[5] The expenditures for measured media in 1961 of other leading stamp companies appear in Table 9 on the next page.

In addition to national advertising, some issuers sponsor local efforts and defray a part of their dealers' costs. These expenditures

Table 9

MAJOR 1961 STAMP COMPANY ADVERTISING (S&H SEE TEXT)

	Newspapers	Magazines	Network	Spot	TOTAL
Blue Chip	$87,937	$ -	$ -	$ -	$ 87,937
Gold Bond	81,110	104,970	-	36,150	222,230
Gold Strike	-	-	-	70,560	70,560
Triple S	-	7,402	-	76,540	83,942
King Korn	36,093	-	-	52,250	88,343
Top Value	172,740	126,817	104,285	207,550	611,362

SOURCES: TvB/Rorabaugh/LNA; ANPA Bureau of Advertising;
Magazine Bureau of Advertising.

TABLE FROM: TV Age, November 12, 1962

are not compiled on an industrywide basis. Sales promotion in the stamp industry takes such forms as direct mail from issuers to consumers, free stamps, and contests. Publicity and community relations are actively employed to build each company's image.

No detail in the stamp process is immune from competition. For example, in the mid-1960's a major company modernized the design on its stamps. At about the same time, many companies redesigned the little saver booklets which are given to the public without charge. One firm's innovation, the issue of multiple denominations, proved practical and the imitators had to revise the layout of their saver books. A more tangible difference among the variegated brands is the number of stamps per booklet. Many books require 1200 stamps; others use 1500 — these sizes are not exhaustive. The most frequent disbursement ratio is 1 stamp per 10-cent sale but some firms have other standards. A few companies tried credit but the public did not want to borrow stamps.

The striving for superiority is particularly pronounced as regards merchandise offerings and redemption-center operations. Many executives explained to the writer why, in their opinion, their company delivers greater satisfactions to savers than other stamp firms. Each company's executives study the catalogs of competitors before they make their moves. Some listings are identical but each firm inserts into its roster some premiums which are of higher quality or higher value per book than the rest of the trade gives. The companies also seek to gain preference for their brand through offerings in greater variety of stylishness and through saver protection against discontinuation or price increases.

It is interesting to compare redemption mixes. The following tabulations show that savers of various leading brands revealed some differences in their choices. Presumably, these contrasts reflect dissimilarity among consumer segments as well as dissimilarity among stamp merchandisers.

Table 10
COMPARISON OF REDEMPTION PATTERNS FOR THREE LARGE STAMP COMPANIES (1966)

Merchandise Classifications	Company "A"	Company "B"	Company "E"
Soft Goods	18.0%	16.0%	20.7%
Furniture	12.5	12.4	6.0
Traffic Appliances	10.5	11.0	4.5
Housewares	9.6	12.0	15.6
Outdoor Accessories	4.0	1.9	3.2
Sporting Goods	4.5	4.8	4.0
Juvenile	3.4	4.5	6.3
Luggage	2.5	1.9	1.4
Bathroom Accessories	2.5	3.2	5.6
Toys	4.0	6.5	8.1
Jewelery and Personal	5.8	5.0	5.0
Tools	1.5	1.4	2.5
Cameras	0.9	0.8	0.6
Clocks	3.4	2.8	2.8
Lawn Supplies	2.1	2.0	1.9
Gift Items	4.1	3.9	7.0
Books	0.4	0.7	0.8
Radios	2.1	3.1	0.4
Silver and Flatware	2.2	0.9	1.0
Glasses and Dishes	2.0	3.6	1.8
Miscellaneous	4.0	1.6	0.8

SOURCE: Premium Practice, March, 1967, p. 62 (Data rounded.)

Another possibility of converting consumers to one's brand is through exclusive or imaginative premiums. Among some novel or creative merchandising by different stamp companies are listings of formal correspondence courses, original paintings (in contrast to reproductions), life insurance, dress patterns, packaged trips, puppies and parakeets, and admission tickets to Disneyland. Some issuers

Table 11
COMPARISON OF REDEMPTION PATTERNS FOR
FIVE REGIONAL STAMP COMPANIES (1966)

Merchandise Classifications	Company "F"	Company "G"	Company "H"	Company "I"	Company "J"
Soft Goods	18.2%	16.4%	13.8%	14.9%	15.3%
Furniture	10.0	9.8	6.0	10.7	10.1
Traffic Appliances	11.4	9.2	12.1	9.9	10.2
Housewares	10.7	12.0	8.7	11.3	11.8
Outdoor Accessories	5.1	4.1	1.3	4.5	6.2
Sporting Goods	4.5	4.0	3.9	4.4	4.0
Juvenile	3.4	4.6	2.9	5.3	4.8
Luggage	3.1	1.6	3.0	3.4	2.9
Bathroom Accessories	3.3	3.5	3.2	4.1	3.9
Toys	4.6	6.5	10.1	4.9	5.8
Jewelry and Personal	4.5	8.5	6.5	4.2	4.2
Tools	3.1	2.4	2.4	2.4	2.0
Cameras	1.9	0.8	2.6	1.5	1.2
Clocks	2.5	2.5	5.4	3.2	3.2
Lawn Supplies	2.1	2.0	0.8	1.5	2.4
Gift Items	3.1	6.5	2.8	4.1	3.0
Books	0.3	0.4	2.0	1.0	1.0
Radios	2.7	0.7	5.2	2.2	1.8
Silver and Flatware	1.4	1.3	1.3	1.8	2.0
Glass and Dishes	1.0	2.1	3.0	2.6	2.3
Miscellaneous	3.1	1.1	3.0	2.1	1.9

SOURCE: Premium Practice, March, 1967, p. 62. (Data rounded.)

tie in with local events such as major-league baseball games.

The public puts heavy pressure on the companies to stock wanted premiums at local redemption centers and to ship special orders promptly. Some issuers have arranged for courses in courtesy for their redemption-center attendants. The issuers encourage the clerks to notify savers promptly when ordered premiums have arrived, to pay attention to unusual requests, and to handle returns or complaints smoothly. Some companies provide special services to eleemosynary institutions. Policies vary as regards cash complements and cash redemptions. Quite a few firms also stock unlisted items at their redemption centers.

At the redemption center the companies strive to provide convenience rather than elegance. They seek accessible locations where parking is easy and the atmosphere informal. A few firms have mobile units or auxiliary redemption stations. Shoppers are invited to browse; some centers have a drive-in service for customers who are in a hurry. This striving to please the saver appears to be general throughout the stamp industry. In the 1963 *Look* Magazine survey, 97% of all stamp savers indicated that they were entirely satisfied with redemption service.° This result seems to be typical. The foregoing sampling from the supply process has pointed to a high degree of competition all along the line. The competitive climate on the supply side has heightened the degree of product differentiation among stamp companies. On the demand side the firms contend with each other and with organizations outside the stamp industry.

Competition for Resources. In the purchase of redemption merchandise, each stamp company's relevant market comprises not only rival stamp houses but all buyers of similar general merchandise. They include discount houses, mail order firms, club plans, variety stores, wholesalers, and others. The merchandisers compete for good values, innovations, exclusivities, and dependable supply. Within the stamp industry, the buying competition narrows down to the relatively few goods handled by the redemption channel. The companies generally stay clear of fads; nor do they use the selling facilities that many manufacturers maintain for other types of merchandisers. The redemption merchandise buyer's particular emphasis is on specialized packaging, catalog allowances, and special prices.

The factor market relevant for the industry also is of broad scope. Stamp companies compete for suitable locations in shopping centers and elsewhere. Besides redemption centers they need warehouse and office space. There seems to be sharp intra-industry competition for managerial, merchandising, and professional employees. Surprisingly many of the officers and middle-management personnel have been associated with more than one stamp company. Within each firm the outlook is parochial. The typical stamp executive is proud of his company and disdains his counterparts in the industry. Policy makers are independent; the largest stamp houses do not even belong to the industry's association. The Trading Stamp Institute of America, Inc., has about thirty-three members (1967).

Except for seasonal accommodations, competition for capital has not been important for most established enterprises. Instead, they compete for investment opportunities. In addition to placing large funds in the money and capital markets, most leading companies pursue active diversification programs. In their product- and market-extension activities one stamp company will often encounter another. For example, all regional and national firms promote vigorously the employee-incentive business, and as another case in point, several American stamp firms have clashed in overseas markets.

Competition for Survival. Thus the trading-stamp business is one in which sharp rivalry is a part of the daily routine. Survival requires strenuous competition for the subscription of new accounts, the brand insistence of savers, and the efficient organization of resources. Almost continually, each company must fend off what Lyon has called "dealer-made laws"[7] plus various harassments mustered by anti-stamp interests, which inject tension and secrecy into each firm's atmosphere. The viable company must find new applications for its services and it must repel substitutes. Although these manifold pressures are strong, the early prospect seems to point toward a state of competition that, in many forms, will become even more intense.

CONCLUSIONS ON INDUSTRY STRUCTURE

The stamp industry has passed through a phase of extremely rapid growth, in large part thrust upon it from the outside, which has altered the structure of the industry. The companies' adaptation under this pressure has been remarkable. The industry adjusted to an explosion in demand coupled with an escalation of legal harassment. There have been no scandals; no known attempts to exploit the stamp for predatory integration; no major conflicts between labor and management; and no startling revelations from the innumerable investigations conducted by various agencies of the federal and state governments. As in any industry, there have been a number of failures but all have been of strictly local scope. Most bankruptcies involved newcomers [8] or retailers [9] who incidentally operated their own stamp plan. The post-Korea history of the stamp industry was exciting but for most large companies it also was profitable.[10]

Whether business is expanding or contracting, there always looms the danger that some day the stamp company's brand may lose its following. But it is not the only danger. If there is a shift in emphasis of economic function — from making retailing more efficient to maximizing the delivery of redemption merchandise to consumers — a major upheaval could ensue. Thus there exists more than one reason why a new test of performance may be at hand.

At the end of the 1960's some expanded stamp companies look as vulnerable as some expanded supermarkets whose stamp has weakened. About 60% of all stamps are sold to food stores. If these stores reduced their usage, many of the associate accounts would drop out very quickly. Such a negative customer-leverage would be amplified financially and operationally. If revenue contracted, there would be a period when redemptions exceeded current cash inflows. Some companies have a thin capitalization; their ability to survive prolonged adversity is precarious.

Most operating expenses would be unresponsive to a downward change in volume. For example, redemption centers, data processing equipment, and most operating staff could not be eliminated (but could perhaps be shared with noncompetitors) if there is a general decline of say, 5 or 10%. A curtailment of customer services would only aggravate the drop. If some companies' officials panic, stamp firms may have to meet desperate price-cutting in order to hold their users, and stamp firms may find that merchandise suppliers are less accommodating than formerly. These vendors may also be less cooperative in proceedings before regulatory commissions and other public bodies.

The Damocles sword of governmental restrictions always overhangs the stamp industry. Furthermore, in the late 1960's the industry could become engulfed by the general trend of legislation and interpretation unconnected with stamps. For example, under a Supreme Court ruling of 1964, joint ventures are illegal if one of its corporate parents would have entered the field individually, leaving the others as significant "potential" competitors. [11] Establishment and enforcement of stricter standards for horizontal mergers could incidentally affect the stamp industry with its continuing trend of consolidations. The United States Supreme Court's stance in 1967 against conglomerate mergers [12] may, in time, block large stamp companies from acquiring nonstamp firms. Similarly the movement in favor of primitive marketing as evidenced by the curbing of advertising in Laborite Britain and advocated under certain circumstances even by the United States Justice Department's antitrust division chief, the enactment of Truth-in-Packaging, and the momentum of such proposals as Truth-in-Lending could possibly deflect into a prosecution of the system. Since the stamp is designed for aggressive businesses, it runs counter the Jeffersonian ideal of a rural economy dotted with small stores.

Numerous Americans, a Louis Harris poll found in 1966, equate middlemen and waste.[13] Also, "it has been almost an article of faith for economists to be highly critical of advertising and to decry it as wasteful . . ." [14] Again, some social critics [15] castigate redemption merchandise as accoutrements of hedonistic living; others begrudge the "common people" the amenities of life. Many persons sincerely dislike the system, and a few opportunists consider it an ideal political target for harassment, if not abolition.

Presumably the companies' executives recognize the risks. Many stamp firms have modern, professional managements. Economists, certified public accountants, statisticians, and lawyers act at the policy level in some companies, not just as specialized staff. Although stamps antedate the 20th century, the expansion in the 1950's brought an influx of youth and new ideas into the industry. The United States Department of Agriculture found that among 108 responding companies, the median corporate age as of July 1957 was 3¾ years. Almost 4 out of 5 companies had been in business less than 10 years.[16] Though now a decade older, these new companies have never weathered a real downturn in stamp popularity.

This is not to predict the direction of stamp volume. The analysis merely points out the danger to the industry if a retrenchment were to occur. Even if that danger never materialized, precautionary action would precipitate a period of hyper-competition. In the end, the well-managed, financially strong, lucky companies will survive, and the industry will be even more concentrated than it is now.

The preceding analysis of the stamp industry's structure has shown that the industry is unimportant relative to gross national product but its output has major significance for consumers, for food stores, gasoline stations, and other retailers, and for manufacturers of premium merchandise. The stamp industry is an open oligopoly with the functions of making certain retail trades more efficient and bringing certain merchandise to consumers. There are substantial differences in price, product, and promotion policies. Although the writer cannot forecast whether future volume will rise or fall, he feels that the industry seems quite vulnerable to any actual or feared upheaval.

"During the past year there has been a great change of opinion regarding Trading Stamps, not only among merchants but among customers as well, and today the better class of dealers who have not stopped using Trading Stamps are preparing to do so, while the more intelligent housekeepers instead of seeking places where stamps are given, as they did a year ago, are now bestowing their custom where this petty imposition is not practiced by the shopkeeper." [17]

The preceding statement was published in 1904. It serves as a sobering reminder to those who foresee an early demise of the trading stamp. Continuity has been the hallmark of the system, and it has achieved a remarkable record during all the changes that have occurred in America since the time when Benjamin Harrison was president.

The stamp industry rose to the challenge of the 1950's. The leading company, under the same family as its original management, changed from a regional stamp firm of small size to an internationally known giant that has diversified into other fields. Its management specifically refused opportunities that could have enabled it to preempt the market for stamps. Instead, other firms entered the industry. Some of the large newcomers are controlled by interests for whom the stamp is secondary. The industry is highly concentrated. There has been one antitrust action but no scandals among the leading firms of this much-investigated oligopoly. But new challenges lie ahead.

CHAPTER VIII

THE STAMP COMPANY AS A RETAILER

This chapter describes the operations of major stamp companies. Their income and outlay are analyzed and compared with other merchandisers in order to isolate economic aspects of the stamp system's role as a channel for certain consumer goods.

REVENUE ANALYSIS

Most businesses have various sources of income, some important and some negligible. Since the inflows are indicative of productive activities, it may be useful to discuss briefly the main types. The stamp system can yield: (1) stamp revenues, (2) financial and contra-operational revenues, (3) merchandise revenues. The main components of these three classes are listed below, and then the distinctive features of the system that they represent will be discussed. Elaboration will be confined to those types that are not self-explanatory.

1. *Stamp revenues*
   a. Transfer of stamps to retailers
   b. Sale of incentive coupons to employers
   c. Delivery of stamps to consumer-goods manufacturers
   d. Sale of gift certificates or stamps
   e. Foreign operations

2. *Financial and contra-operational revenues*
   a. Interest on float
   b. Lost stamps
   c. Catalog allowances
   d. Financial dealings with users or vendors
   e. Subleasing of data processing equipment, space, etc.
   f. Return loads in own trucks
   g. Disposal of old fixtures or other fixed assets
   h. Sales tax commission (from state)

3. *Merchandise revenues*
   a. Sale or leasing of stamp dispensers
   b. Leasing of elaborate signs
   c. Sale of goods for cash to the public
   d. Sales to employees
   e. Liquidation of close-outs

Stamp Revenues. In the above listing, "retailer" means anyone deal-ing directly with the ultimate consumer, including transportation com-panies, institutions, and other organizations that contract with an issuer for disbursement of the gift to their direct customers. The transfer of stamps to retailers is an issuer's main source of revenue. In the mid-1960's the industry's average price per stamp was about two mills, equal to ten dollars per pad of 5,000.

During the past ten years there has been a steady decline in the industry's average realization per pad. In the first place, the customer mix changed from low-volume, high-price outlets to supermarket chains. Second, the industry grew in size and experience, and realized many external and internal economies. Third, the advent of captive stamp companies after 1955 may have exerted pressure on the pricing decisions of independent companies. Finally, rivalry has increased, not only among stamp brands but also through substitutes. In the early 1950's tape register plans, premiums, and similar counter moves usually were not effective but in the late 1960's some contests and discount operations were.

In sum, while demand for stamps was climbing rapidly and most forms of promotion became more expensive, the issuers lowered prices to their clients. For example, The Sperry and Hutchinson Company divulged to this researcher that in 1953 its average price per pad of 5,000 stamps was $12.80; by 1963 it had shrunk to $11.15.

Countering these forces toward price reduction have been the high proportion of stamp redemptions and the high values offered to savers. "A consumer redeeming S & H stamps in 1953 received merchandise worth about $1.04 for stamps, the use of which cost the merchants $1. In 1963, the consumer's merchandise value was about $1.16 for every $1 of stamp cost to the merchant."[1] The merchandise values quoted are regular retail prices, not manufacturers' list or suggested prices, according to S & H's chief executive officer.

Four other channels of flow are identified in the category of stamp revenues. One of the industry's most vigorously promoted forms of diversification is the sale of incentive coupons to employers as awards to personnel for outstanding performance. Meredith points out that the lack of continuity is a major handicap of this activity.[2] Neverthe-less, incentive coupons may be highly effective in motivating work-manship and punctuality among savers and extra selling efforts among the husbands of savers. If, however, the stamp company must install extra facilities and provide special merchandise for a limited program, it is doubtful that its capability for this type of service is superior to incentive specialists.

The use of stamp coupons as pack-ins by various manufacturers of consumer goods used to be a much larger part of the market in the decade before and after World War I than it was during the 1950's. In the 1960's, some coordinators sell stamp coupons to non-competing manufacturers. Since large producers of consumer goods like cigarettes and foods sell their brands nationwide, whereas most stamp brands circulate regionally, the participating issuers allow the consumer to exchange the pack-in for any eligible stamp brand. This form of external product differentiation [3] is used also with a single, national brand. The issuer transfers its stamps to packers of consumer goods such as hardware and notions. The packers assemble and package the goods and stamp sheets; then they wholesale the combination to retailers.

Smallest in volume is the sale of gift certificates and stamps to consumers. Such direct sales can injure the issuer's major users. It may be surmised that due to the stamp's gratuity image, gift certificates on redemption-center merchandise would have a limited market.

The last source of revenue listed is foreign operations. A few independent companies are selling stamps to retailers in Japan, United Kingdom, and other foreign markets. In addition to the usual impediments in international trade, American corporations have met with the same type of adverse stamp legislation abroad as in this country. Moreover, in countries which do not have antitrust laws, product differentiation and sales promotion may be less important. [4] Thus in the late 1960's the main source of stamp revenues is proceeds from retailers, and the basic retail outlet is the supermarket.

Financial and Contra-operational Revenues. These proceeds are buttressed by various kinds of financial income and expense-offsetting items. With respect to credit, the stamp plan has the interesting feature of converting what is usually an expense into a revenue. Most issuers do not extened deferred terms to users. Instead, the stamp house receives the cash some six to nine months, on the average, before redemption. This advance collection provides the company with a float available for productive investment.

In contrast, many discount houses are financially over-extended. After the mid-1950's a number of prominent (and lesser) discounters went into bankruptcy or merged into other corporations. With debt too high relative to net worth and profit margin too low to improve it, many discount houses are in a financial squeeze; merchandising operations are conducted in an atmosphere of perpetual crisis.

The stamp firms can systematize their process; cash receipts are at the beginning, not the final stage. Most of the industry's users are outlets whose seasonal fluctuations are quite mild. Like a life insurance company, the stamp firm enjoys a fairly regular inflow of cash throughout the year.

After stamps have been issued there is a progressive build-up followed by successive deceleration in presentation rates. In other words, the stamp company's redemptions in any year are attributable to a portion of the current year's proceeds plus a portion of past years' proceeds. Some modern companies estimate this distributed lag actuarily: they construct mortality tables based on a sample of stamps returned by savers. The tables show the time pattern of tenders and the percentage of survivors (stamps not redeemed). One procedure for "aging" a sample of booklets and estimating call rates is explained in a recently completed manuscript.[5] This article also describes an accounting technique of matching revenues with expenses.

The difference in timing between proceeds and redemptions is bridged by a liability account. There are basically two ways of matching revenues with expenses: (1) defer the recognition of revenue or (2) anticipate the incidence of expense. Each method can be accomplished through a variety of acceptable procedures. For example, some companies reserve for the cost of merchandise only; others reserve for the expense of maintaining redemption facilities as well. The reserve percentages also differ among companies because their redemption rates and accounting policies are not uniform. Some issuers have accumulated reserves longer than others. The percentages vary from year to year for any one company, depending on whether volume is rising or falling. During a period of sales expansion, tenders may drop below 90% of current issues. During contraction, redemptions may exceed 100% of current revenue.[6] Thus the stamp process has a contracyclical feature which acts as a minor stabilizer in the economy. Although these variations preclude direct comparison among companies, an idea of the relationships between revenue, redemption reserve, and net worth within some corporations may be gleaned from Table 12 which shows estimates for 1965 or thereabouts.

It appears that many companies' reserve approximates 50% of annual sales. When sales are fairly stable, they will automatically replenish the issuer's cash, so that the redemption reserve can produce

Table 12
ANNUAL SALES, RESERVES FOR UNREDEEMED STAMPS AND
OWNERS' EQUITIES OF SELECTED TRADING STAMP COMPANIES

Corporation	THOUSAND DOLLARS			Year Ended Or Date	Footnotes
	Estimated Revenue	Liability for Stamp Redemptions	Owners' Equity		
The Sperry and Hutchinson Company	$330,610	$158,195	$93,040	1/1/1966	(7a)
Top Value Enterprises, Inc.	123,573	79,133 (7b)	9,101	3/26/1966	(7c)
Blue Chip Stamp Company	80,915	50,000 (7f)	18,000 (7f)	2/29/1966	(7d)
E. F. MacDonald Stamp Company	58,857	27,880	3,604	1/31/1966	(7c)
King Korn Stamp Company	23,932	14,400	1,146	7/31/1965	(7c)
Stop and Save Trading Stamp Corp.	15,000(7f)	6,173	6,121	2/27/1965	(7e)
Merchants Green Trading Stamp Co.	15,000(7f)	8,007 (7g)	2,633	5/1/1965	(7e)
Holden Trading Stamp Company	4,976	4,913 (7h)	2,326	1/30/1965	(7c)
Gold Bell Enterprises, Inc.	4,710	2,185	(18)	12/25/1965	(7c)

Due to differences in accounting methods the data are not comparable.

Footnotes 7a to 7h in Appendix form a part of these data.

interest continuously. In practice, many companies invest part of the float in their own operations.

The industry's growth of the 1950's provided opportunities to compound the float. As long as sales rise, calls for premiums will lag and the fund of prepayments should increase. In the case of $1,000 annual net additions for a dozen years compounded continuously at 4% annually, a fund grows to $15,324 — not just $12,000. This statement is general as to amount but not as to percentage or time. Net annual increments of $1,000,000 at 4% yearly result in $15,324,000 in twelve years. At higher interest rates or for longer periods the sum would grow substantially larger; at lower rates or for shorter periods it would be much smaller.

And, inevitably, some stamps will never be presented. Even United States paper currency is lost or destroyed at an estimated 0.1% annually.[8] More typical and relevant, perhaps, the housewife must pay for 1.18 pounds of fresh tomatoes harvested for every 1.00 pounds bought at the store. The difference is lost in packing and through spoilage.[9] Since a substantial percentage of all food bought is not eaten, the actual spread between cost and consumption is wider yet. Nonutilization is neither unique to the stamp system nor, according to various estimates, extraordinarily large.

The writer made a financial survey of the industry. Among the larger companies responding, all reported redemption percentages in the 90's. According to a recent state government report, small firms are likely to experience a lower rate than large companies, because the small issuer's retailers and delivery facilities are fewer and more widely scattered.[10] But this inference might not be correct. In fact, it is prohibitively expensive to project the ultimate percentage except on a sampling basis because complete analyses of redeemed books to determine the issue dates of the contents would cost far more than the books are worth. The true experience is known only when a company goes out of business and a termination date on its liability is set.

A respondent to the writer's financial survey wrote that he had sold his company with the proviso that the successor would be reimbursed for as many of the $550,000 worth of outstanding stamps as the public would present within two years. "Since both the name and the color were changed at the time of the sale, this was a perfect test on redemption that I thought would be of interest to the study you are making. The two-year period ended October 1, 1965, and we are approximately 99.2% redeemed on all stamps that were outstanding," he stated. Data on two larger companies are gleaned from the forementioned legislative study which noted that the Ed Schuster Company redeemed 99.5% of its issues over thirty years and the McKelvey Company, 98.2% over forty years.[11] This report also cited a 1960 United States Tax Court decision that placed the redemption figure of Frontier Saving Stamps, Inc. at 95%;[12] the same rate at which The Sperry and Hutchinson Company settled with the Internal Revenue Service. It takes many years before actual utilization can be closely approximated.

A moderate rate is not necessarily a waste although, of course, it could be such. If consumers do not avail themselves of the stamp's conversion power, the brand is ineffective, and the user should discontinue it. But, instead of general apathy, a stabilization of tenders below 90% of issue could reflect consumer heterogeneity. In the latter case, the forfeitures can be deployed toward higher premium values; they may be the stamp company's means to fasten to its users the allegiance of an important buying group of avid savers. This is exactly the situation — the existence of a small, strategic class of savers — that a motivational researcher has hypothesized.[13] But desirable stamps somehow do find their way to a redemption center, and premature actions based on current data may be risky. Consumer research is especially important if the redemption rate appears to be changing.

The issuer may be torn between striving for the highest possible redemption rate or trying to get by with a lower one. A moderate rate can bring greater immediate profit, a lower price to users, and a higher value to active savers. A high rate engenders mass support which is the most persuasive influence on retailers that deal with the general public. The executives who were interviewed stated that their strategy was the latter — a high redemption rate. Some of them felt that most stamps not tendered by holders represent a lag rather than a loss. One executive cited the unexpectedly high presentation of stamps to a large user-issuer after its stamp-issuing subsidiary had been discontinued.

Another, relatively minor, source of revenue is the catalog allowance that many manufacturers grant to mail order houses. Some stamp firms consider the catalog allowance a reduction of their Cost of Redemptions. But in terms of its purpose, the catalog contribution could be classified also as advertising allowance which is an offset to Marketing Expense. This is the treatment used in the data at the end of this chapter. The other expense-mitigating items listed are incidental. They comprise necessary activities subsidiary to a company's main business function and productive uses of temporarily idle resources. This section on financial and contra-operational revenues has dwelled at some length on certain ramifications of forfeitures and reserves because there seems to be widespread interest in these features. The next group of revenues is of lesser importance and will be mentioned but briefly.

Merchandise Revenues. The final class, merchandise revenues, is small in amount for most issuers. More than one-half of stamp supermarkets employ dispensing machines. Some issuers charge their customers for such equipment and for displays. Finally, one of the problems of catalog houses is an inventory of goods whose listings are not renewed. Although stamp companies try to emphasize continuity, they may discontinue one-third or so of their listings after a catalog has expired, partly because manufacturers change their models. The disposal of obsolete merchandise is the last source of revenues mentioned.

These various elements have been listed to convey an idea of the scope of revenues. Some classes are nominal or nonexistent for most stamp companies. A few result in losses when costs are considered.

EXPENSE ANALYSIS

The next section shows the deployment of the revenues discussed above. It will describe the selection of redemption merchandise, followed by analyses of redemption-center maintenance, marketing efforts, and administrative operations.

Concentrated Variety. One of the advantages of the stamp channel is the economy of offering and handling narrow assortments of a wide variety of goods. Yet the super-skim-scrambled merchandising system is not without problems of its own. The hybrid nature of the stamp channel also carries over into its operations. The issuer is both a catalog house and a retail chain.

Since the customer who has saved stamps toward a specific premium has no alternative source, inventory adequacy is critical to good stamp saver relations. Hence a company's objective is continuous availability of most listings, at the booklet-price shown in the catalog, in each of the redemption stores. This necessitates, for example, an alignment of every manufacturer's model cycle with the company's own catalog period. It requires very close estimates of each center's demand for every listing, with protection against interruptions in supply and against cost increases.

A stamp company seems to have the pick of the fastest moving items among any kind of merchandise but in reality its choice is circumscribed in many ways. Trade executives feel that some savers plan toward a particular item and that many listings should follow behind the fashion trend. The fact that selections must be made one and a half to two years in advance of an annual catalog's expiration date almost guarantees such a lag. On the other hand, the executives also realize that some savers look for the latest small appliances or other novelty to distinguish themselves as a taste leader. The redemption center often stocks many items in addition to the catalog listings; it is sometimes used for testing new articles. Wares that are not suitable for a redemption center can still be moved to savers through manufacturers' drop shipments. Further, the stamp company can contract for repair service on major appliances. But ordinarily the company must exclude perishable goods, extra-heavy or bulky merchandise, articles that are bought in many different sizes, fashion goods, complex equipment requiring service. It cannot list job lots or manufacturers' close-outs because there is no assurance of continued availability. Furthermore, it does not want to invite accusations of offering inferior selections.

Since a special trip for an inexpensive item is not worth while for the saver and a very expensive listing entails too long a delay, the majority of the articles are in the over $2.50 to less than $9.95 retail range. Goods subject to resale price maintenance are preferred. Most stamp companies emphasize well-known brands of merchandise to give savers an assurance of recognized quality. The offering of presold goods may increase a stamp brand's appeal and reduce the company's risks but it also narrows its choice.

In the short run, the capacity of existing redemption centers limits the size of the line. The demand for some listings is confined to a certain season or region. This further reduces the effective breadth of the offerings. Another limitation is the need to enlist local support against the attacks by anti-stamp groups. The judicious purchasing department places business in every section of the country where its company operates. Policies on foreign goods differ; some firms virtually exclude imports whereas others romanticize a few exotic features.

The issuer's challenge is to assemble an attractive merchandise line in spite of these restrictions. With a following in some 80% of all local households, the stamp firm must project a general appeal. A feel for the type of goods selected by stamp savers is conveyed by the following tabulation. As computed by *Premium Practice*,[14] a simple average of the merchandise delivered in 1966 by America's ten largest stamp companies showed, in addition to 2% miscellaneous, the following twenty categories:

Soft goods	16.7%	Sporting goods	4.3%
Housewares	11.4	Clocks	3.2
Furniture	10.2	Luggage	2.5
Traffic appliances	9.2	Glasses and dishes	2.3
Toys	6.3	Radios	2.3
Jewelry and Personal	5.5	Tools	2.2
Gift items	4.6	Silver and flatware	1.5
Juvenile	4.4	Cameras	1.3
Outdoor accessories	3.9	Lawn supplies	1.8
Bathroom accessories	3.6	Books	0.8

Catalogs merchandise good living. According to the 1963 National Appliance Survey sponsored by *Look* Magazine, the stamp industry purchased some 29% of all electric clocks, 10% of all automatic coffeemakers, 13% of all toasters, and 8% of the steam irons shipped by American manufacturers.[15] In addition, stamp houses feature lamps, hassocks, silverware, and bedspreads. In full view and frequent use around the home, the premiums remind and motivate the consumer to continue saving.

The stamp company envisions an "average" home owner whose tastes are middle-of-the-road. Universality and versatility are the main criteria in the selection from eligible merchandise. Buyers seek something functionally superior to what the "average" housewife might get for cash but they shun cost-boosting attachments. The listings must conform to a catalog's theme, such as "Modern Living" or "Traditional America." Some items in higher-priced lines or for specialized taste may be included if they do not disturb the sense of unity. The ideal listing is a leading seller (in the conventional market) of a type used in households, of long-established or rising popularity, and harmonious in various decors. There are a few instances of listings that have been continued without change for a decade or longer and whose redemptions have kept pace with the newer items in the catalog. The perennial favorites buttress the image of continuity. On the other hand, the time lags in the process may also require that a listing be discontinued after it seems to have passed its peak, even though it may still have a following.

Buyers scan shelter magazines and trade journals, observe fashion trends and analyze manufacturers' opinions, visit trade shows and factories, note special requests from redemption centers, keep an eye on competition, and generally try to screen all that might fit into their catalogs. There follows a series of progressive eliminations until a few candidates are selected for physical inspection and value analysis. For example, the writer visited a sample room during the week when it was allotted to lamps. The company lists some forty-five numbers in its catalog, of which perhaps fifteen were slated for replacement. The final round had narrowed down to about 300 lamps. In addition to the general suitability of the product, a merchandiser must consider its cost-price relationship and approriateness for his operation. With uniform catalog prices wherever it operates, the stamp company ought to use total cost delivered to the consumer as the financial criterion.

A manufacturer who sells a substantial part of his output to a stamp firm can easily customize delivery and packaging to the buyer's needs. But a stamp company's preference for nationally known manufacturers limits the feasibility of modifications, and it may be necessary to pay extra for arrangements that minimize total cost. On the other hand, the number of vendors from whom a stamp house buys merchandise is less than one thousand. The transactions are large. The combination of selectivity and quantity makes for personalized relationships.

Some vendors can pass certain cost savings on to the stamp company. The buyer does not take point-of-purchase materials, advertising mats, mailers, detail men who arrange stocks and count inventories in retail stores, demonstrators, and similar services. Stamp companies are usually a vendor's house account because they buy once a year a limited number of items in very large volume. The issuer's predictable redemption pattern may enable a manufacturer to reduce his production cost. Manufacturers of branded goods help their *conventional* retail accounts by designing the latter's materials handling and merchandise display methods, training their personnel, surveying their customers, counseling their executives, designing their accounting, and providing various other services without charge. In some lines, push-money (manufacturers' payments to retailers' salesmen), is general practice.[16] None of these expenditures applies to the stamp house. Hence it is not surprising that many manufacturers categorize the latter as a distinct customer class for pricing purposes.

As explained previously, the financial flow in the stamp system enables the going concern to discount its invoices. The manufacturer saves the expenses of special dating, extended billing, floor plan financing, or allowance for bad debts.

These various cost savings and additions result in a basis to which the stamp company executive adds a mark-up of a uniform percentage. He tests whether the prospective listing meets the issuer's standard of retail value. Executives from several companies who were questioned all stated that they set redemption prices to assure a value of three dollars per book in actual retail prices. Pricing practices differ, of course. In some cases the catalog allowance granted by some vendors may be influential. Most issuers try to feature at least a few leaders priced below the listings of rival stamp companies. Additional modifications, for standard intervals such as one-quarter or one-fifth book and for other purposes, may be necessary.

To a theorist like the writer it seems that the price-setter should consider the elasticity of demand. Implicitly, stamp houses do so when they list small appliances and some other goods at rates on which they generate large volume even though they can be spectacularly undersold by conventional retailers. But this result appears to follow more from pricing-policy rigidity than sophistication. In view of the long experience with a limited number of articles, it would appear that there must exist profit opportunities in economic pricing that some issuers fail to exploit. On the other hand, elasticities differ over time and place. The life and dispersion of the catalog crimp the economic-pricing proclivities of the company's executive committee.

If the sample under consideration for a listing passes the merchandising and financial criteria, the buyer for the company must negotiate a dependable supply for the catalog period. Every listing is critical and ties up the stamp house while its catalog is in circulation. Thus the channel captures many benefits from the concentrated variety although, inevitably, it also carries some penalties. A department store may offer one million different items[17] and can replace them in response to fads and seasons. The catalog house lacks this kind of flexibility.

It is this inherent inflexibility, however, that sets the stage for many cost savings. Predictable operations can be planned in depth and controlled for maximum efficiency. From the time that an article is first selected for a listing to the ultimate redemption by a saver, the administrative fulcrum is "packaged quantity."

Cost of Redemptions. The logistics behind the caption "cost of redemptions" will be described, with special emphasis on the unusual disadvantages and advantages of stamp houses. In addition to the factory-cost of the merchandise the caption includes the expenses of landing it at the redemption center and releasing it to the saver. The typical sequence is: manufacturer—transportation company—stamp company's distribution center—internal handling and storage—truck redemption center.

The stamp company must balance the relative costs over the entire delivery process. With respect to the outer container, the objective is to minimize total landed cost to the redemption center. Ideally, the individual package should correspond to a listing, thus obviating assembly or break-bulk when it is handed to the saver. Unless manufacturers' direct shipments to the redemption center or consumers are efficient, a double cycle is used. The manufacturers' goods are shipped to a distribution center whence the requisite quantities and assortments are delivered once or twice a week to each nearby outlet.

The facilities of the stamp firm's private carriers, warehouses, and redemption centers can be customized because the product line is narrow and the operations are relatively stable. The company's engineers and merchandising experts may redesign a product to make it more functional for the consumer and cheaper to land at the redemption center. Thus the stamp company contributes form utility. When it first lists an item, the organization must fill the pipelines; then an automatic reordering formula helps guide the replenishments. Inventory control—using packaged quantity as the unit of account—may be computerized. A computer program helps determine the ideal packaged quantity in the first place, including the size and color assortments. Because of this consistency, engineers can devise the most efficient methods of unloading, palletization layout, materials handling, storage, and loading. For example, a certain six-million cubic foot warehouse through which a tow conveyor moves 9,750,000 pieces of merchandise per year is a base for more than 100 redemption centers. Aisles are a mere 6 feet, 6 inches in width—just enough to accommodate a forklift truck that stacks the merchandise up to three floors high. Bridges across the aisles provide additional storage space.

This type of equipment and the warehouse's layout are suitable only for light merchandise. If the stamp company's line were more varied or its volume more unpredictable, a more flexible staging area would have to be organized. It would be much costlier. This is one of the handicaps that plagues the conventional retailers. The stamp firm's quality control may function at two levels. The mass receipts are sampled at the warehouse, and the small population is checked at the redemption center for conformance to specifications.,

As a result of the trading-stamp channel's selectivity its merchandise turnover can be much higher than the department store's but this advantage is offset, to a large extent, by the requirement of stocking the numerous redemption centers. In 1966 the merchandise turnover of The Sperry and Hutchinson Company was 5.2 times which compares favorably to the about 3½ number of stock turns (at retail) reported by department stores.

Redemption Center Expenses. The evolution of redemption facilities shows the continuing effort to serve stamp-collectors efficiently. Before the turn of the century the independent companies operated premium parlors where the saver was shown the kind of goods that he might order. Most of the selections were one-book items, and some companies gave premiums for as little as twenty-five or forty-eight stamps. Broadening their scope, some companies opened order offices for arranging redemptions by mail. User-controlled firms and also some independents operated in-store order desks or redemption stations. Either the retailer's or the stamp company's personnel staffed the in-store redemption centers. Subsequently, the companies set up separate stores, with an area of perhaps 5,000 square feet, of which one-third was for display and two-thirds held reserve stock. Stamp companies stressed personal service.

The mass influx of savers in the 1950's pressed on the capacity of these conventional units, and some companies devised means to shorten the queues. Many centers instituted express lanes for savers who called for a single premium. Another method was to designate one station for ordering, and another for the delivery of the incentive via conveyor belt. Increasingly, the redemption process changed to self-service.

This trend toward self-service in redemption centers necessitated special fixtures, special packing, and special displays. Larger show rooms were built. The newer stamp salons averaged perhaps 8,000 square feet. In the few places where the self-service concept has been almost completely implemented, the proportions allotted to display and storage were reversed, 2:1. Some companies feature drive-in windows and some have mobile units.

In the mid-1960's the industry employed all of these types of facilities. Delivery of the merchandise to the saver typically occurs at a small store, with perhaps 5,000 to 10,000 square feet of space, usually not in a high-traffic location. Most companies prefer a site near a major user where they can provide parking space, but not in the busiest section of town. Such a location makes it easier for the saver to take his premiums with him and it allows an atmosphere of informality.

Secondary addresses are less expensive than prime, of course. But since the redemption store may draw perhaps 65,000 savers and browsers annually, some developers have offered stamp companies substantial concessions to rent in their shopping centers. Hence stamp stores are also to be found at the most desirable locations, either because they are invited on favorable terms or because local conditions require an expensive address.

It is the more prevalent transaction locale, the ordinary store-like redemption center, that invites comparison with general-merchandise discount stores and department stores.

In the usual type of redemption center about two-thirds of the area consists of storage space where leasehold improvements and public facilities are virtually nil. In contrast, the typical discount store allots 22% to storage.[18] The smallest volume class or department store in the NRMA survey allots 32.4% of its space to nonselling activities; the largest, 47.0%.[19] Large department stores need manufacturing rooms for upholstering furniture, altering clothing, repairing jewelry, and preparing food for restaurant departments. A large amount of space is occupied by elevators, escalators, and chutes. The department store may provide special staff and space for check-cashing services, parcel checking, and adjustments. It allots floor space to public telephones, rest rooms, and other conveniences for the general public. Most redemption centers provide none of these services and incur none of these expenses.

The stamp company also minimizes seasonal decorations, window display by professional designers, and similar retailing expenses. A redemption center's merchandise-selection and pickup station is functional; it is neither shabby nor elegant. In some cases the display area is carpeted, decorated, and heated or airconditioned.

A redemption center's annual volume averages about 140,000 books (basis 1200 stamps). Not only are the stamp company's facilities smaller than those of most other mass merchandisers but also the redemption center's hours are much shorter. This results in lower labor costs and lower operating expenses. When the stamp store is open, the space has a relatively high utilization rate. The value of annual transactions approximates $62 per square foot of total area which is higher than the $53 rate reported by *The Discount Merchandiser* for the average nonfood discount house in 1964. On the basis of *customer* area only, the same source placed the nonfood discount house at $66 per square foot. The N.R.M.A. survey resulted in an average of $80 sales per square foot. Using 1963 United States Census of Business data as the basis for all stamp company statistics in this section, the writer adjusted for nonredemption and for the average relationship of retail value to stamp revenues, and found the redemption center's utilization rate to be an equivalent of $184 per square foot of customer area. In this respect the redemption center is more than twice as efficient as conventional outlets.

The supervisor of a redemption center often is a woman with administrative ability and clerical experience. She may have one or two counter girls and a stock boy. The attendants are likely to be more informative to the consumer about the relatively small number of premiums than are the sales personnel of a large conventional store about its offerings. In the Census, the average number of employees per redemption center was 3.9 persons; average wages per employee came to less than $60 per week. Of course, redemption stations do not need highly paid executives and staffs. But a large general-merchandise chain pays its store managers a salary averaging close to $20,000 per year.[20]

A premiums outlet ordinarily has no cafeteria facilities, employees' lounge, or library, but labor relations within stamp companies have generally been good. The closely-knit group sustains few stock shortages, but there are some. There is little repricing of merchandise; markdowns by S & H, for example, amount to 0.3% of catalog value. Total shortages and markdowns reported for a regional sample of self-service discount houses, 1963, was 5.6%.[21] In the same year, markdowns and stock shortages in department stores amounted to 7.4% of net retail departments' sales.[22]

Redemption store employees have a service, not a selling, job. Perhaps three-quarters or more of the patrons know in advance what they want to get. On average, each redemption center employee delivers the equivalent of $117,000 worth of goods to the consumer. By way of comparison, the annual volume per department-store salesperson was about $27,000 in the smallest class and $49,000 in the largest, according to the National Retail Merchants Association.

The stamp industry's average redemption is about two and one-half books at 1,200 stamps, or two books at 1,500. One company's president wondered whether 3,000 stamps was a magic figure. Magic or not, these withdrawals represent a much higher retail value than the average transaction of $5.25 in a discount house and $5.79 in a department store.

Nationally, the stamp industry has one outlet per 25,000 stamp-saving households. Because of the multitude of brands the ratio overstates the availability of redemption centers. On the one hand, most people do not save all the locally available brands. On the other hand, the more brands each household does save, the greater the number of patrons served by a redemption center. The ratio of households per discount house is 19,000:1 and per department store, 17,600:1.

If there is no redemption center near the saver's home, he can get his premiums by mail. But only a tiny percentage of redemptions is accomplished via this method. Most savers accept the premiums at a nearby outlet. Usually no gift boxes or special wrappings are supplied.

The stamp store operates on a "redeem-and-remove" basis. It has no delivery service and no credit and collection expenses. In contrast, a typical department store makes 60 per cent of its sales on credit.[22] In the pure stamp operation, clerks do not cash checks or make change. The clerks inspect and count saver books. The personnel holds the books for auditors who reconcile the stamp receipts and supervise their destruction. The rate of merchandise returns is very low since fashion goods are generally avoided, and losses to the stamp firm are minimized through adjustment procedures pre-arranged with the vendor. In sharp contrast to the cost advantages at the redemption stage is the special outlay for marketing service to consumers and users.

Marketing Expense. The saver who enters a redemption center has been presold by the company's catalog. In fact, the issuer relies on its catalog as a major initiator and sustainer of the stamp habit. Free dissemination of catalogs is a very costly burden. In recent years, catalogs have become more elaborate and hence more costly because of growing competition within the industry, compounded by mounting difficulty to enlist new savers as the pool of households abstaining from stamps declined. A very large stamp firm's cost of a catalog is about seventeen cents per copy. A medium-sized company's catalog expense is a few cents higher. Collector books are about a cent each, and stamps cost about eighteen cents per pad to print, according to trade sources. These expenses are miniscule in comparison to the outlays of big merchandisers like Montgomery Ward & Company whose expense for publishing catalogs runs close to two dollars a copy.[24]

The catalogs of major stamp firms are sumptuous promotional pieces in four-color rotogravure, with a generous proportion of blank space to print. Covers are plasticized. Not only has the quantity printed become larger and the presentation more elaborate, but also the typical catalog has become much thicker since the early 1950's. For example, in 1950 The Sperry and Hutchinson Company published 21 pages featuring 242 listings; in 1960, 95 pages with 1,054, and in 1967, 186 pages with 2,007 listings. A part of this expansion reflects a growth of the redemption line, and a part is a shift toward a more complete listing.

A catalog has certain indivisibilities which inhibit the stamp house. To add two or three listings overall is difficult, since it is not possible to annex one page. The minimum physical addition in most bindings is four pages; the minimum that is financially feasible may be higher yet. This limitation could be overcome by varying the dimensions of the catalog. But with its emphasis on continuity, the sensitive merchandiser hesitates to deviate from an established format. An executive from a medium-sized firm disclosed that his company publishes catalogs at the rate of one per three saver-books redeemed. Seven saver books are printed for every four currently redeemed, he added. The production of a catalog entails, of course, the familiar expenses of paper stock, models, editorial writers, creative services, illustrations, and printing. The distribution of a catalog entails shipping it to licensees and redemption centers plus promoting its placement into the consumer's hands. Trade sources estimate that in 1967 some 100 million trading stamp catalogs were received by United States consumers.

The necessity to keep the stamp unit of account stable in the face of the deterioration of the dollar unit limits the life of a catalog. As a byproduct, monetary inflation accelerates the filling of stamp books, and the offering must be continually upgraded. In the mid-1960's some companies listed premiums worth one hundred books or more, and redemptions were high enough to warrant the listing.[25] Most catalogs are valid for about a year. A new edition ordinarily adds many new items or models but perhaps two-thirds are carried over, which may eliminate a portion of the catalog expense. Some regional and local stamp companies "syndicate" their catalogs — they use common pages with companies in other areas—for greater buying power and lower production cost.

The catalog is the keystone of the stamp company's promotional effort to the consumer. It may be supported by advertising in all types of media plus sales promotion such as direct mail and free stamps plus public relations. Although directed primarily at the consumer, the promotional efforts also pave the way for negotiating franchises.

The solicitation of stamp users can be classified under selling of intangibles, one of the most difficult challenges in business. In a very large stamp corporation before a sales campaign is planned, an economist studies the potential of an area. Marketing research may precede the actual approach of an important prospect. The results of the survey are lettered on graphic displays for use by a marketing consultant and a sales executive in a formal presentation to the prospect's top management.[26] The important customers are house accounts. Once affiliated with a stamp brand, they are likely to continue for a long time.

Associate accounts turn over at the rate of once every three to five years, depending on company policies and local conditions, according to some executives. These smaller companies are signed up by salesmen who handle perhaps 100 to 150 of such associate accounts. A large issuer maintains headquarters, regional, district, and zone offices for successive levels of sales management and for storage of selling materials. In 1960, S & H zone managers typically had yearly earnings of between $10,000 and $17,000. Local salesmen earned, including commissions, $8,000 to $12,000, once they were established in an area.[27] Established accounts are serviced periodically. They receive free display materials, saver books, signs, and the salesmen give advice and make adjustments. The company may encourage its sales personnel to participate in local affairs. It may be active in many community affairs, seeking to earn a favorable reputation among local officials and citizens. Thus the stamp company incurs many marketing costs for promotion to consumers and users. In addition, there are the normal administrative activities such as general management, accounting, insurance, personnel services, and legal counsel.

Administrative Expenses. Under this heading are subsumed all of the familiar general and staff functions. To put them into context, it may help to visualize the stamp enterprise as a highly dispersed sales and branch-store operation. Hence there is a need for managerial and accounting controls including internal audit. Local distribution of payrolls and local stamp security require formal procedures as do the protection of fixed assets and merchandise. Another practice in the industry is a "close audit" of large customers' books in order to verify their liability to the issuer under a flat percentage-of-volume contract.[28] But, in general, the simple nature of the trading-stamp process limits the requirements on accounting.

Like all retailers, a stamp firm must cultivate a favorable image at the local level. Large companies use local bank accounts, join local chambers of commerce, and contribute merchandise to local causes. These expenses are part of a coordinated public relations program. The corporation also must qualify in every state and comply with various laws and ordinances wherever it does business, as customary in interstate commerce.

In addition, the industry has been under frequent attacks, often instigated by commercial opponents of trading stamps. The intensity of the assaults is an indicator of stamp effectiveness. A company meets these attacks through research and education. These terms have broad meanings. Research is a multi-purpose activity. Finding a better way to serve users or savers or vendors or some other group of citizens may be a basis for justifying the system during some proceeding. Education includes communicating this news as well as other facts about trading stamps. Publicity, lobbying, institutional advertising, and other informational services all are embraced in this term.

In early 1967, several bills had been introduced in the Congress and others were pending in fifteen state legislatures. This volume was small in comparison with previous years. Because the basic contentions have not changed much since the turn of the century, the legal staff or outside counsel experiences a learning-curve effect.

Personnel administration is conducted in a manner similar to other large retail chains. This brief description has sketched the functions financed by administrative expenses.

FINANCIAL SUMMARY

Compared to general retailers, the trading stamp industry is diminutive, yet it is large enough to act as mass distributor of a limited number of goods. This specialization enables the stamp house to develop many efficiencies in the deployment of goods for a predictable pattern of demand. Labor expense, for example, is relatively low. Large companies like S & H, Top Value, and MacDonald usually incur about 11% of sales for personal-service compensation; the department-store average is 17%; discount houses are generally inbetween. Moreover, the trading stamp process generates extra revenues which bolster the issuer's ability to provide its savers with good value. On the other hand, the channel is burdened with higher marketing and legal expenses than conventional retailers.

Can a financial statement highlight these channel differences? This concluding section of the chapter presents a comparison of margins between The Sperry and Hutchinson Company, the largest of the stamp firms, and and typical department stores. S & H data for 1963 were recast by the Company to parallel as nearly as possible the "All Department Stores" margins furnished by the Controllers' Congress of the National Retail Merchants Association. No comparable survey of discount-house statistics was found. Even the N.R.M.A. data shown in Table 13 and elsewhere in this chapter are an aggregate of many diverse operations and therefore not an entirely valid reference. Differing conditions and accounting methods always impair the comparability of any such sets of data. With these limitations in mind, one can examine the assumptions and results.

When merchandise is roughly similar but the prices of two distributors differ, as in the case of S & H and department stores, expense percentages by themselves are apt to be misleading. A sound analysis must equate merchandise moved to consumers, then compare distributor revenues and costs. Efficiency thus depends on what the distributor moves to consumers compared to what he gets, spends, and earns.

This information is provided in Table 13. In a study of premium values, to be described in Chapter X, a book of S & H stamps averaged $3.29 in terms of regular department store prices. (S & H's occasional markdowns — which raise the value of a book to $3.30 — are disregarded, for the sake of simplicity). The Company disclosed that it collected $2.68 per 1200 stamps, on average. This leaves an extra value to savers of $0.61 per book to be explained in the Margins Analysis of Table 13.

The two columns at the right give the percentage breakdowns of the merchandise value shown in the first column at the left. When a customer buys an article for $3.29 at a department store or a saver redeems such an article for a stamp book at an S & H Center, what are the main elements of these equivalent values?

First, the value of $3.29 is reduced by the department stores' total markdowns to the special-sale price of $3.09 which is really unnecessarily low (see Chapter X). There remains a difference between the average value given at special sales prices, $3.09 per book, and $2.68,

Table 13

COMPARATIVE MARGINS AND CONSUMER VALUES
S&H AND DEPARTMENT STORES
1963

S&H Values Per Book		OPERATING MARGINS S&H	Dept. Store
	SUMMARY FINDINGS		
$3.29	Average Department Store Value per Pricing Study		
2.68	S&H Net Sales Revenue per Book Issued		
$0.61	Extra Catalog Value to Savers		
	MARGINS ANALYSIS		
$3.29	Regular Prices in Department Stores	100.0%	106.0%
.20	Department Stores Markdowns	6.0	6.0
3.09	S&H Book Value After Markdowns	94.0	100.0
.14	Stamps Not Expected to be Redeemed	4.3	
2.95	Net	89.7	
.27	Apparent Channel Efficiency	8.2	
2.68	S&H Net Sales Revenue per Book Issued	81.5	
.14	Add Back: Stamps Not Expected to be Red.	4.3	
2.82	Revenue per Book Expected to be Redeemed	85.7*	
1.79	Landed Cost of Goods	54.3	65.1
1.03	Gross Profit	31.4	34.9
.29	Store Expenses	8.8	17.9
.19	Administrative Expenses	5.8	8.1
.32	Marketing Expenses	9.7	3.7
.80	Total Expenses	24.3	30.2*
.23	Operating Profit	7.1	4.9*
.06	Other Income/(Loss)	1.8	(0.3)
.29	Income Before Taxes	8.9	4.6
$0.15	Net Income	4.5	2.3

* Rounding or weighting variance

SOURCES:

S&H Data: Corporate Research Department, The Sperry and Hutchinson Company, New York. Used by permission.

Department Stores Data: Controllers' Congress, National Retail Merchants Association, New York, Used by permission.

the average amount collected by the stamp company. If S & H is charged for unredeemed stamps assumed at 5% of issues, the residual is whittled down to $0.27. This $0.27 per S & H book appears to be a channel efficiency — a superior performance to society of 10% on the stamp company's revenues — subject to qualifications noted at the end of this section. First, the rest of the operating statement will be interpreted.

Since S & H can dispose not just of the proceeds for its stamps but also of the 5% not expected to be redeemed, the latter is added back to derive total revenue per book expected to be redeemed: $2.82 (85.7%). Subtracted from this revenue is the wholesale cost of goods and the expense of getting them to the selling floor. For department stores this item — landed cost of goods — absorbs 65.1%; for S & H, 54.3%, of retail merchandise value. Thus The Sperry and Hutchinson Company, based on its large volume of purchases and its integrated wholesaling function, achieves on its somewhat similar products a substantially lower cost.

Likewise, in the operation of stores, the S & H expense ratio is much lower than in the case of department stores, 8.8% against 17.9%. As pointed out earlier in the chapter, most redemption merchandise is presold by its catalog and requires relatively little labor cost, compared to department stores, to sell on its premises. The average transaction is higher for S & H than for department stores which also contributes to lower labor expense. Again, there are fewer stamp company services — no credit and delivery, for example. As to Administrative Expense, S & H is again lower, about 5.8% versus 8.1% for department stores, reflecting economies in managing a very large and highly standardized mass distribution system.

On Marketing Expense, however, S & H is substantially higher than department stores, about 9.7% against 3.7%. This disadvantage to S & H arises from the cost of running the stamp side of its business— its selling effort, catalog, collector books, stamps, advertising, and the like. Since the department stores' Marketing Expense is net of cooperative advertising allowances the S & H percentage was likewise netted.

Proceeding down Table 13, one notes that compared to department stores, S & H enjoys a unique nonoperating income — the yield on its investment of reserves for outstanding stamps. This amounts to approximately 1.8% of the merchandise value that the stamp company distributes. When this small offset and all the above-mentioned expenses are taken into account, there remains a profit before taxes for S & H of 8.9% of merchandise redemption value compared to only 4.6% for department stores. Taxes reduce both ratios by approximately one-half.

Thus the stamp distribution channel as exemplified in this study of S & H emerges as a very efficient system by the standard of department-store operations. Consumers actually receive on average higher merchandise value through redemption than the payment by contracting retailers when they acquire the stamps. Of course, such a conclusion is subject to qualifications. The author has not allowed a discount for licking and sticking of stamps, waiting until books are filled, nor for less variety of choice than department stores offer and the fewer services provided by redemption centers.

The S & H Company is not only efficient; it is also profitable. Extending the 1963 comparison to S & H's unadjusted balance-sheet[29] and income-statement[30] data, one can compute return on investment as follows:

Formula:	$\dfrac{\text{Pretax Earnings}}{\text{Sales}}$		$\dfrac{\text{Sales}}{\text{Capital Stock and Surplus}}$		$\dfrac{\text{Pretax Earnings}}{\text{Capital Stock and Surplus}}$
S & H:	9.76%	X	3.75	=	36.60%
Department Stores:	4.61%	X	3.09	=	14.68%[31]

This stamp company's profit margin is double the average department store's. After S & H's profit margin is levered by a somewhat higher turnover of owner's equity, it results in a return on investment two and one-half times the department-store average. Interestingly, the assets turnover is 2.11 times for department stores and only 1.19 for The Sperry and Hutchinson Company. The stamp firm's Total Assets base is high because one-half is not merchandising facilities; it is in the form of Marketable Securities, apparently for the protection of savers who have not tendered their Green Stamps as yet. When these two items, the securities and the liability for stamp redemptions, are eliminated, the company's assets utilization is in line with department stores'. And the sales/working capital ratio shows S & H ahead 9.30 times to 4.07.

Although minor differences could be accidental, such large magnitudes between S & H and conventional channels strongly support the impression of stamp-channel efficiency. In any event, before the conclusion of superior performance is accepted, the results of research on stamp companies' merchandise value must be examined. Available information on various surveys will be reviewed in the next chapter. It is followed by a chapter in which the author's investigation of S & H redemption-merchandise value is reported.

CHAPTER IX

PRIOR STUDIES OF STAMP BOOK VALUES

Thus far the study has presented an analysis of trading stamps and traced their receipt by savers from contracting supermarkets, gasoline stations, or other users which, in turn, had acquired them from a member of the trading-stamp industry. The issuers operate redemption centers where the process draws to a close.

The value of the premiums that savers obtain at these redemption centers is the subject matter of the next two chapters. It is a topic with a highly controversial history. For example, *The Journal of Commerce* reported in 1915: "Practically every coupon and trading stamp institution offers commodities that are not up to standard grade in quality."[1] This was contradicted by The Sperry and Hutchinson Company which during the same year had published that one book of their stamps costing the retailer $2.275 was good for some premiums with a retail value of $3.25 and some at $3.75. And in the following year, the United States Supreme Court castigated devices such as trading stamps which "by an appeal to cupidity lure to improvidence."[2]

But instead of examining these old disputes, this chapter will review some estimates of stamp-book values made in the past decade. These estimates can be found in the literature or in the private files of the researchers. A review of some of these studies follows. The Sperry and Hutchinson Company released two of its unpublished surveys, which will be noted.

PRICING STUDIES USING SMALL SAMPLES

Agricultural Marketing Service Study. In 1957 the United States Department of Agriculture published the results of "a small pricing study" made in Washington, D. C. in November 1956 by its staff.[3] The stamp book employed in this connection required 1,500 stamps for completion, not 1,200 as in the case of the S & H book whose value will be discussed in the next chapter. This difference in the denominator can be bridged by using average rates of return. The rate of return is the average retail price of a premium divided by the consumers' total outlay for goods, based on an assumption of one gummed token for each ten-cent purchase. If, for example, with

Table 14

RATES OF RETURN ON PURCHASES VIA TRADING STAMPS FOUND BY AGRICULTURAL MARKETING-SERVICE IN WASHINGTON, D.C., IN NOVEMBER, 1956

Item	Number of Stores	Average List*	RATE OF RETURN Department Store	Discount House
Steam - Dry Iron	14	2.49%	1.64%	1.64%
Portable Mixer	13	2.49	1.69	1.60
Automatic Toaster (A)	12	2.49	1.69	1.67
Roster Oven	6	2.31	1.75	1.63
Automatic Toaster (B)	5	2.49	1.80	1.80
Aluminum Dutch Oven	3		2.71	
Dictionary	2		2.22	
All Items Priced	25			
Median Value		2.51	1.99	1.67
Range in Value		2.31 - 3.43	1.13 - 2.83	1.55 - 2.29

* At the time, dealers in many states had to maintain list prices but merchants in the District of Columbia did not.

SOURCE: U. S. Department of Agriculture, "Trading Stamps and the Consumer's Food Bill," Marketing Research Report Number 169, Washington, U. S. Government Printing Office, 1957, p.6.

$1,000 expenditures for food, gasoline, etc., the customer receives stamps entitling him to a premium that would have cost $20 in a department store or discount house, the rate of return is 2%.

For 25 items an Agriculture Department researcher found the median rate of return based on department-store prices to be 1.99%. Two additional rates of return were 1.67% in discount houses and 2.51% according to manufacturers' suggested retail list prices. The original work included rates of return in its presentation. Table 14 (page 114) gives the Agriculture Department results, with no change other than to present them in descending order of "number of prices found."

Presumably the seven items tabulated were only part of the research since twenty-five items were priced. The Agricultural Marketing Service pointed out that "this small study shows the possibility of wide variation in the money value of a book of trading stamps." They also noted that "the items selected for pricing were those most likely to be found in department stores and discount houses. As a result proportionately more electrical appliances and housewares were included in the listed prices than are usually found in stamp catalogs." The United States Department of Agriculture conjectured that "this bias does not appear to be too important . . ." [4] but it is doubtful that this assumption is correct.

An inspection of their data, arrayed in Table 14 by number of times priced, clearly suggests a tendency for wider availability of an item to reflect adversely upon the value given by the stamp company. One would, however, need a far larger sample to test this relationship. The rate of return on the most frequently found item was 1.64%; on the two least frequently found items it was 2.71% and 2.22%. This relationship is true even in similar products. Toaster (A) and Toaster (B) both had the same manufacturer's list price. Toaster (A) was located twelve times and had a 1.67% rate of return; Toaster (B) was found only five times and had a 1.80% rate.

When the Department of Agriculture data are separated by product category, it is evident that the five small appliances are substantially below the two other items. Put most dramatically, the two non-appliances had a value 44% higher than the small appliances! Such a ratio is an invalid exaggeration, however, because the sample is too small and lacks representativeness.

A number of conclusions can be drawn. The data showed a relatively low money's worth per book on small appliances or on merchandise which is widely available. Incidentally, an analysis of the Agriculture Department table also reveals that the price difference between department stores and discount houses is largely attributable to product mix. Out of the total difference of 0.26 percentage points between store types shown in Table 14, all but 0.04 points are due to the additional items priced in the department stores. Since the study encompassed only four department stores versus thirteen discount houses, it also shows that the latter carry relatively few — and an unrepresentative few — of the goods listed in a large stamp company's catalog. The study also points up the large variation that occurs even in such a limited search. The range for department store returns was almost as large as the median value itself.

Other Published Estimates. Another test of stamp-book values appeared as a small part of a 138-page study, "Trading Stamps" by Brian J. Strum, published in December 1962 by the *New York University Law Review.*[5] The author chose nine items "simply because they were in the catalogs of at least two of the stamp companies."[6] But, in his view, "since each company offers over 1,500 different items . . . because of the limited number of samples [the] analysis cannot be indicative of competition among stamp companies."[7] Nevertheless, he had no qualms about offering his "department store price" on nine items as a means of comparing the claimed and actual values of redemption merchandise. Although he asserted that five of the stamp plans have national distribution, he gave one department store price for each item. Is he implying that retail prices are uniform? For example, in Strum's test "the" price of a General Electric iron works out to the equivalent of $1.98 per book of S & H Green Stamps. In contrast, the study discussed in the next chapter found that an iron in the then current catalog ranged in value per book from $2.11 in one city to $2.92 in another — and this span is merely suggestive of the wide price variability of a single article among different retailers. But in Strum's article, price consists of a single amount.

If the characteristics of redemption merchandise values noted in the Department of Agriculture survey are relevant, the reader would probably predict that a selection of widely available small appliances and high-cost goods would yield atypically low values per book. The Strum study exemplifies this.

In another example, a Kiplinger publication presented two charts which converted stamp-catalog listings, mainly of small appliances, into price "charged by a typical metropolitan discount house."[8] Not surprisingly, the values per book were low and were used to warn of the hidden cost of stamps. A sample of items representative of consumer redemption choices might not have yielded so dramatic a result. The brand of stamp was not identified. Another estimate is mentioned in a footnote of a widely circulated article by two professors.[9] The full description of the redemption-value portion of the study reads as follows: "The value of the trading stamps issued for the case study store was determined. Items in the stamp catalog were priced in several outlets and an average value per book of stamps was computed to be $2.66. The range in value per book of stamps varied from $1.96 to $3.37 depending upon the item "purchased" with the filled books." [10]

In correspondence with the author, Professor William H. Wallace revealed that his sources were "various mail order catalogues such as Sears, Wards, Spiegel and Milway and others . . . [plus] department and discount stores . . . As I recall there were about forty items in the sample . . ." The professor added: "There was no consistency between the various stamp catalogues as to which was higher or lower on any particular item." [11] This statement contradicted his published work on the study, reproduced above, which reported that only one brand of stamp had been evaluated.

In further correspondence Professor Wallace added the following recollections concurred in by Professor Bromley:

"1. We did not consider delivery charges when using mail order catalogues because some of the items were priced at local discount houses.

"2. The sample comprised about 40 items, not all were available in each stamp catalogue, but had to be in at least three.

"3. The items in the sample seemed to be fairly diversified realizing a majority of items could not be used because of a lack of identification. Most of the items comprised of luggage, small appliances, camera equipment, pots & pans, shavers, card tables & chairs, flatware, clocks, shot guns.

"4. Four of the five stamp companies (national) only one was local and has since failed." [12]

Other Tests. Two other estimates are mentioned in the literature screened. A study by Dean Weldon J. Taylor and Associates of

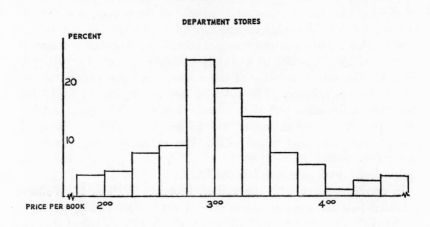

Figure 3

DISTRIBUTIONS OF PRICE PER BOOK
BY STORE TYPE

DEPARTMENT STORES

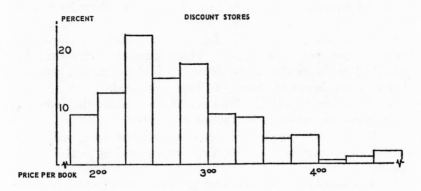

SOURCE: The Sperry and Hutchinson Corporate Research Department.

Brigham Young University [13] found values per book for S & H of
$3.19 at department stores and $2.44 at discount houses in the state
of Utah. The other test, noted in a study by the Midwest Research
Institute, resulted in a value of $3.06 per S & H book in Montana
in 1962. [14] These two estimates offer additional price evidence from
particular states.

Different stamp companies naturally may offer unlike levels of
value. S & H, for example, has claimed in its advertising to offer more

value than its competitors both in terms of merchandise and other attributes. Thus it would not be surprising if studies of various brands were to arrive at different value levels. This is particularly so since the issuers sell their services at different prices.

UNPUBLISHED S & H DATA

Two pricing studies made by The Sperry and Hutchinson Company for internal purposes are available for comparison. One was conducted at The May Company, a department store in downtown Cleveland. Briefly, 295 items were priced in February 1960; the result was an average (arithmetic mean) value of $3.00 per book of S & H Green Stamps. The spread of values for individual items was between under two dollars at the low end and over five dollars at the high. Thus, even in a single store in a single city, there was a vivid display of variability, assuming that the items were correctly identified.

The other pricing study was made in mid-1963 when S & H merchandise managers obtained actual retail prices for items in four cities at department and discount stores. They located 761 articles in department stores, weighted the prices in proportion to estimated redemptions, and found an average department-store value of $3.06 per book. The weighted average for 276 items found in discount stores was $2.71. Combining these two figures proportionately to the number of items located, one arrives at a weighted single estimate of $2.98. Although such a combining procedure is not rigorously accurate, it may give an indication of overall value. Figure 3 shows the wide range of individual prices found as well as the tendency for discount-house prices to concentrate in merchandise with lower values per book. Thus, although the overall means in both studies were near $3.00, the details show a wide range of prices.

LARGE RETAIL SURVEY

An article published in 1965 was entitled, "The Value of Trading Stamps as Measured by Retail Prices" by Harvey L. Vredenburg and H. Howard Frisinger. Since the senior author of that article had, in 1956, published the most comprehensive and penetrating academic study on trading stamps ever written, his name promised a high standard of scholarship. In the work under discussion, he and his colleague, an assistant professor of mathematics, fulfilled this expectation.

Recognizing the problem of price variability within and among items, the two professors sought to develop "adequate methodology for determining the value of a stamp book"[16] so that it would represent all the items in the book in direct proportion to their popularity or redemption rate and at the various prices at which they might be found in the monetary market. Based on redemptions in the Denver area, they drew a stratified random sample of 100 items from an S & H catalog. In the summer of 1964 the two professors and six graduate and senior students made an exhaustive canvass of the Denver area — more than 300 stores were visited. On each item found the professors computed an average (arithmetic mean) price per book; then they weighted these means by strata and computed an overall mean. Table 1 from their report is reproduced as Table 15 below.

The study reports, for the eighty items located, an average value of $3.11 per book. Seventy items located in department stores averaged $3.21 per book versus $2.82 for fifty-two in discount houses. This disparity in number of items suggests that some of the price difference is due to product mix as well as item-by-item price differences.

The table also shows prices for additional items not actually found in stores and for which considerable effort was made to obtain accurate quotations or buyers' estimates of prices if the items had been carried. The average value per book for these items was higher than for those located, suggesting that a sample estimate of equivalent book value understates true worth to the extent that it is influenced by the widely available, competitively priced articles.

A segregation by merchandise category in the study reveals a spread of values from $2.47 for small appliances to $4.38 for lamps. The two professors commented: "Items that are traditionally retailed at relatively low mark-ups (small appliances, linens and blankets, and sporting goods, for example)"[17] tend to represent a lower value per book of stamps. Conversely, lamps and silver appeared at the high end of their list, representing the superior values given by the stamp company.

The writers concluded that "there was considerable variation in stamp-book value, depending upon the merchandise selected by consumers. Selection of a certain single item resulted in a book value as low as $2. The best value resulting from a single selection was $5.88. The median was $3.06 and the middle 50 per cent ranged

Table 15

RETAIL VALUE OF COLLECTOR'S BOOK OF 1,200 RPD STAMPS *

	TRADITIONAL STORES		DISCOUNT STORES		ALL STORES	
	Number of Items	Weighted Average Value**	Number of Items	Weighted Average Value**	Number of Items	Weighted Average Value**
Located and Priced in Denver Stores	70	$3.21	52	$2.82	80	$3.11
Not Found in Denver Stores But Estimated by Experienced Store Buyers***	26	3.40	29	3.26	19	3.46
Total	96	$3.34	81	$3.02	99	$3.21

* Fictitious name. (The actual subject of the study was S&H Green Stamps.)

** The weighted average is derived by weighting the average value for each stratum in proportion to actual redemptions in Denver.

*** Estimates were calibrated by having buyers estimate book values for items where retail prices where known. In this way, tendency to overestimate or underestimate could be controlled.

SOURCE: Table 1 from report by H. Vredenburg and H. H. Frisinger published in Journal of Retailing, New York University, Fall, 1965.

from $2.53 to $3.40." Since this survey was conducted in only one city area, the variation excludes any that might occur among cities across the nation.

SUMMARY

The estimates of stamp-book values published during the past ten years are not strictly comparable because they have covered various stamp plans, different cities and, most important, unlike methods. There are, however, some common tendencies.

The study described at the beginning of this chapter dealt primarily with electric appliances and housewares and therefore produced low average values. Researchers at the Department of Agriculture explicitly called attention to the limitations in their survey, even those limitations that they considered unimportant. Some other published estimates reviewed in this chapter dealt with even more biased samples, but their authors failed to note that findings could not be generalized. Where wide varieties of items were priced, values were generally close to three dollars per book. Because only S & H was identified in most of these latter cases as the subject of the study, this value can only be generalized to S & H, on the basis of the research cited.

By contrast with most other studies, the Vredenburg-Frisinger research may well serve as a model for estimating the value of a stamp book. It was, however, confined to the Denver area and thus does not represent a "national average." Its value finding (for S & H stamps) was about $3.11 per book. In the next chapter this result will be compared to a broader, more recent, test.

CHAPTER X

RETAIL VALUES OF S & H STAMPS

This chapter tests one aspect of company performance. It reports a field survey which endeavored to ascertain the value at retail of merchandise which the consumer obtains when he redeems a book of S & H Green Stamps. It was found that the average premium's value is about $3.25 per book. This exceeds the stamps' average cost to users by 21% but both averages have wide dispersions.

PURPOSE AND PROCEDURES

In order to obtain a fair and representative estimate of the value of a trading stamp book, the writer undertook a probability — sample pricing study in various cities throughout the United States. A sample was used because pricing the entire two thousand items would be unduly costly and might, by the sheer size of the task, yield no greater reliability than a well-drawn sample. The objective was to determine the retail price that consumers were paying in the cash market for the merchandise that savers were currently electing to procure with stamps. Since the redemptions are priced in units of filled stamp books, the field study also used the latter as a denominator. The value obtained could then be contrasted with the dollar cost of the same quantity of stamps to the retailer. The difference would be either an excess for the consumer or a deficit.

Definition of the Sample Space. Ideally, for such a study, the conventional market should encompass every retail outlet in the United States where premium-type merchandise is sold. Nobody knows all of these retailers or the sales rate of the catalog items in each of the hundreds of thousands of stores. Precise definition of the stores to be sampled will require some limitations on these broad markets.

It would have been desirable to price the catalogs of all stamp companies. In order to weight the values appropriately, however, it would have been necessary to get each company's estimate of current redemptions. A request for this confidential data was broached to a number of companies. When the largest firm, accounting for an estimated 38% of all stamp sales, agreed to supply its data the writer decided to measure their value since it could be considered modal for the industry.

The frame that was desired in order to sample and stratify the items was actual current redemption figures but the lag involved in getting such figures would mean that weights and prices would not be matched in time. The latest available redemption data would have reflected the experience of the 1964 period. A 1966 survey based on them would have necessitated sampling from an outdated catalog containing obsolete items. Rather than try to price obsolete premiums — with the problems of estimating and substituting that might have arisen — it seemed preferable to work on the basis of the current catalog, current merchandise, and current company estimates of redemption volume.

The company whose catalog was being priced has considerable experience in estimating its redemptions for its own planning purposes. Not only is a correct forecast crucial during its catalog year but the company's policy against merchandise cash sales or close-outs is verification of its ability to gauge the popularity of its items. Although some items had been overestimated in past forecasts, others had been underestimated. Examination of records indicates that there is no tendency for these over or under-estimates to be correlated with value, and therefore it was believed that the list of estimated redemptions could be employed with confidence.

Paramount Principles in the Design. Two considerations governed the sampling procedure. First, neither the researcher nor any party at interest should have any influence over which article was included or excluded. Membership in the sample should be left to chance. Second, subject to this restriction the composition of the sample should have a high likelihood of being representative of the choices made by stamp savers. The opportunity for inclusion should be proportionate to total volume of books redeemed for each item. These considerations dictated that the research (1) meet the statistical requirements for randomness and (2) employ the principle of stratification.

Methodology. As the actual survey plans were drawn several choices were made. The population was narrowed to the listings in the current catalog of The Sperry and Hutchinson Company, the

Ideabook. It was decided that the retail market could be adequately represented by a canvass of large discount and department stores. These were to be located in six geographically dispersed areas, each serving a city among the fifteen largest cities in the United States.

The survey sought to answer the following question: What is the equivalent price of a book of S & H Green Stamps? The general method used was to select a sample of listings from S & H Catalog No. 71 and to have them priced in retail stores. A median value per book was obtained for each item located. These medians were weighted to reflect the item's popularity with savers and then averaged to obtain an overall average value per book.

Sampling Procedures. The sample of items to be priced in the full-scale survey represented all listings appearing in the May 1, 1966 *Ideabook* which shows merchandise redeemable for S & H Green Stamps through April 30, 1967. The sample was drawn from a listing representing projected redemptions.

The sampling frame enumerated all *Ideabook* listings in descending order of total book redemptions. Successive deciles of these redemption totals defined ten strata. Thus, Stratum I consisted of forty articles which accounted for the top 10% of redemptions. Stratum II accounted for the next 10%, and so on. The last segment, Stratum X, contained 799 items. With the help of a random numbers table, a random sample of twenty items was drawn from each of the ten strata for a total of 200 items in the sample.

The actual pricing of these items was done in the late summer of 1966 by the professional staff of Andrews Research, Inc., of New York. The cities selected were: New York, Detroit, Minneapolis, New Orleans, Philadelphia, San Francisco. In each area the shoppers were to search at least two large department stores and two large discount houses, with half the shoppers canvassing department stores first, the others beginning in the discount houses. Shoppers were provided with pictures and descriptions including model numbers where applicable of the items to be located and were instructed to price these specific items only — not technological or other substitutes. Shoppers were asked to obtain one price per item and to concentrate additional effort on finding other articles rather than additional prices for the same item. While multiple prices per item might have provided a check on market-price stability, and indeed some shoppers recorded prices of the same article found at more than one store, it was felt that the primary effort should be directed toward obtaining prices for as many wares as possible. The local supervisors verified prices on 5% of the goods. All original field data were delivered to the author for editing, tabulating, and further processing.

Survey Results

Summary. The shoppers located a total of 129 different items (64.5%) out of the 200 sought. Seasonal factors, model years, and other limitations prevented finding the balance. Overall average value per book came to $3.25 at regular retail prices. If sale prices had been used, a slightly lower figure might have resulted.

This amount, $3.25, is significantly greater than the $2.68 average paid by retailers for the equivalent number of S & H Green Stamps. The strata averages varied from $2.87 to $3.71, with half of them between $3.15 and $3.25. The median value per book for individual items ranged from a low of $1.58 to a high of $6.72 with 76 of the 129 items (59%) between $2.50 and $3.50.

There follows a detailed description of average values and the methods used to obtain them. The sources and significance of the wide variation in the values found for individual articles are discussed in later sections. A detailed examination of the nature and representativeness of these responses was part of the analysis and is also reported subsequently. Numerical estimates of the value per book per item and the methods used to arrive at them are considered first.

Value–Median per Book per Item. The first effort was directed toward obtaining a representative value per book for each item priced. When the survey was planned it was decided to use the median of all the prices obtained for any one article divided by the number of stamp books required to redeem it to arrive at "value per book per item." It may be easier to visualize this simple equation in the following form:

$$\text{An item's value per book} = \frac{\text{Median of that item's prices}}{\text{Number of books required}}$$

No attempt was made to distinguish between department or discount store prices. Presumably equal effort was made to obtain prices from both types of stores — each was visited first by half of the shoppers. Also, what was sought was a representative measure of the regular price at which the item was readily available to a mass of consumers, without regard to the sources or any extra (missing) services or conveniences (inconveniences) which might come with it.

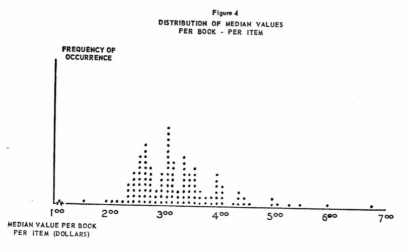

Figure 4

DISTRIBUTION OF MEDIAN VALUES
PER BOOK - PER ITEM

The median (the middle value) was selected as the appropriate statistical measure because of the nature of the data and the statistical attributes of the median. A set of price data usually tends to be positively skewed—i.e., it tends to stretch upward. When plotted it has a long tail extending toward higher prices. By the same token, it has an absolute lower limit at zero. Figure 4 shows the general shape of the distribution of the prices found for the present survey data. The data tend to cluster around $3.00. While one might have found retail prices as high as $6 or $9, one could not have found any below zero. Since the median is not readily influenced by extreme values, it is considered appropriate for these kinds of data. The arithmetic mean (sum of all the values divided by their number), which takes into account each observation *and* its distance from the center of gravity, is more easily influenced by any occurrence of extremes. By the same reasoning, if there were any errors in pricing made by the field force which were undetected either by the field supervisors or by the editing, they would not have as drastic an effect on a median price as upon an arithmetic mean.

A comparison of the median and the mean for the seventeen items in Stratum I which were successfully priced is shown in Table 16. The table shows that in fifteen of the seventeen articles the median

Table 16
COMPARISON OF MEDIAN AND MEAN FOR STRATUM I

Item Number	Median Value per Book	Arithmetic Mean Value per Book
00	$2.44	$2.39
01	3.15	3.36
02	3.32	3.76
03	2.61	2.61
04	4.07	3.99
05	3.70	3.70
06	2.75	2.75
07	2.56	2.56
08	2.40	2.44
09	2.44	2.47
103	6.73	6.73
104	4.98	4.98
105	2.65	2.70
106	1.95	1.95
107	3.82	3.82
108	3.07	3.11
109	3.38	3.38

Arithmetic Mean: of Medians $3.295   of Means $3.334

was equal to or less than the arithmetic mean. Thus, as was expected, the median proved to be the more conservative measure and was used to obtain the "value per book per item."

Value—Average per Stratum. After a satisfactory measure of value for each item was determined, the values for all goods in a stratum were averaged to obtain a value per book for each stratum. In this case the arithmetic mean was used for the "average."

In contrast to the individual prices, a less skewed distribution was expected of the medians. It also seemed desirable to give full weight to each median without any attempt to minimize the effects of extreme values. A table of the means of the median values for each stratum follows.

These means are plotted in Figure 5. There is a noticeable consistency among the means for the various strata which is observable

MEANS OF MEDIAN VALUES FOR EACH STRATUM

Stratum Number	Mean of the Item Medians
I	$3.30
II	3.12
III	3.16
IV	3.27
V	3.19
VI	3.47
VII	2.87
VIII	3.07
IX	3.71
X	3.31

Mean of Medians: Weighted = $3.247 = $3.25
Unweighted = $3.249 = $3.25

in the table or the plot. In statistical terms, 95% confidence intervals constructed for each of the stratum means were found to include the overall mean. Glancing down the list of stratum means, one notes that whatever variation there is appears to occur randomly over the strata. There is no pattern in which the average value per book increases or decreases with the popularity of the items. The mean of the median values for Stratum I was $3.30 and for Stratum X, $3.31.

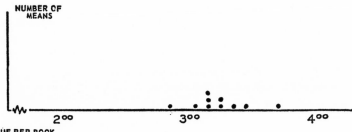

Figure 5
DISTRIBUTION OF STRATUM MEANS

NUMBER OF
MEANS

MEAN VALUE PER BOOK
PER STRATUM

Value—Overall Average. To obtain an overall average value per book the means of the strata were weighted by their proportional share of estimated redemptions and summed. Since each stratum was designed to represent 10 per cent of the total estimated redemption value, the medians were each multiplied by 0.1 and summed. Obviously, this procedure was numerically equivalent to obtaining the arithmetic mean of the stratum means; i.e., adding them together and dividing by ten.

The weighted mean value per book obtained was $3.247. To check on the effect of weighting, a simple arithmetic mean of the item medians was computed. When the median values per book for all items were summed up and divided by 129, it was found to be $3.249. The similarity in results obtained by using the weighted mean or the simple mean confirms the impression that there was little difference among strata and thus the weighting by stratum did not affect the computed values. Whenever it is deemed important to emphasize that the value per book found reflects the choices of the savers the weighted mean will be used even though, when rounded, it happens to be indistinguishable from the simple arithmetic mean of the median values.

Statistical Significance of the Mean. Since an average retail value per book was obtained which is higher than the average dollar amount paid for an equivalent quantity of stamps by the contracting retailers to The Sperry and Hutchinson Company, the question arises, "Is this difference real?" The mean retail value per book was obtained from a sampling study; the difference from users' cost could be a reflection of sampling variation rather than a true difference in value. It is thus necessary to compare the $3.25 with the $2.68 average cost incurred by the merchants for a book of stamps.

The statistical problem could be phrased: Could $3.25, the mean of the sample medians, have come from a universe of values whose true mean value was $2.68? The difference between the two values was found to be significant at the .01 level, so the hypothesis that $3.25 came from a universe whose true mean is $2.68 was rejected with 99% confidence. This sample survey offers evidence that the average retail value per book redeemed by the saver is significantly higher than the sales proceeds received by Sperry and Hutchinson.

THE DISPERSION OF PRICES

By determining a representative value per book the major goal of the sampling study was accomplished. But in addition to information made available by locating the center of a distribution, much can be learned from examining the dispersion of the data. Since the median prices were widely spread (Figure 4), the analysis was extended. The Company's average sales proceeds of $2.68 were compared to the distribution of all median prices. It was found that only thirty-five individual medians (26%) out of the 129 fell below that mark. With only 26% of the items below the $2.68 level, the saver receives extra value for his stamp book in most of the articles he chooses. The spread found was from $1.58 to $6.72 per book. A more detailed look at this range and the reasons for it follows.

Table 18
AVERAGE VALUE PER BOOK BY CLASS OF ITEM

Class of Item	Number of Items	Average Value for Class
Small Appliances, Radios	21	$2.62
Bath Shop Items	8	2.92
Luggage	4	3.02
Linens	12	3.06 *
Sporting Goods	4	3.11
Tools	4	3.19
Housewares	11	3.20
Toys and Juvenile	10	3.24
China	5	3.31
Furniture, Lamps	21	3.49
Picnic and Garden	8	3.45
Jewelry and Clothing	10	3.95
Silver, Hollowware and Flatware	4	4.13
Miscellaneous	7	3.67
	129	

* Average value for towels and sheets only - $2.76.

Differences—Among Merchandise Categories. The dispersion noted was traced to various sources. The first one—merchandise categories —is presented as Table 18. It shows the mean value for fourteen classes of premiums, classified so that none contains less than four items. The average values per class range from $2.62 for small appliances and radios to $4.13 per book for silver, hollowware, and flatware. This variation is in line with previous findings, particularly the detailed Vredenburg-Frisinger study. The survey results imply that, over a period of time, pricing policy has differed systematically between the dollar and the stamp channels. The latter is not competitive on articles sold for example, in "August White Sales" or at large discounts. These noncompetitive items are the types of goods that are widely available in conventional channels and widely priced as leaders.

This relationship between low mark-up and intensive distribution in the cash market emerges from an analysis of the goods that were priced most frequently. Although the emphasis in this survey was on obtaining only one price per item per city, some shoppers recorded additional prices on easily located items. All items located five or more times — two were found as often as nine times each — were segregated and their medians examined. The medians for these twenty frequently found items ranged from $2.44 to $5.20. This last item and one other whose median was $3.97 were the only two of the 20 articles whose value per book were above the survey average. The other 18 frequently found items were below the average value.

It follows that a store type or a city in which relatively more of the widely available merchandise was located is likely to show a lower overall stamp value level than another. As was discussed in the previous chapter, many prior studies confounded differences in availability of goods with differences in prices.

Differences—Among Store Types and Cities. In the present survey, the items found *both* in department stores and in discount houses were segregated. The resulting average values per book for these thirty-seven items were $3.05 for department and $2.79 for discount stores. This spread of about 7% is smaller than the difference between the average value per book for *all* items found in *either* of the two store types. A simple compilation of all prices, classified by type of store, yields a mean of $3.29 per book for department stores and $2.88 for discount houses. The larger spread is a product difference, not a store difference. It reflects the fact that the canvassed discount houses did not carry the types of goods that, for various reasons, have a higher value per book in the cash market, and that department stores did not carry the very low value-per-book items.

The test shoppers had been instructed to record the customary prices of the articles but, of course, retailers always feature some kinds of specials. Hence the recorded prices reflected any regular adjustments; temporary discounts were excluded. On the average, in department stores, markdowns come to 6.0% of original retail;[1] markdowns average 3.3% in discount houses.[2] Although perhaps excessively harsh on the stamp channel, a reduction of the values per book from regular prices to average special prices may be estimated as follows:

Value per Book of S & H Green Stamps	Department Store	Discount House
At regular prices	$3.29	$2.88
Average markdown in nonstamp channels	.20	.10
At special sales prices	$3.09	$2.78

This analysis was not carried further since it violates two of the major premises of the survey — to price items readily available to shoppers without regard to source and without regard to time. The process of weighting by redemption patterns precluded studying department and discount stores as separate sources. And since most redemption merchandise is readily available throughout the catalog year, regular prices were studied rather than those which might prevail for a limited "special sale" period.

On a city basis, the same differences obtained. In the city where the percentage of items located was the highest, the average value per book was the highest also. The spread of book values on a city basis again reflects differences in both product mix and actual prices. As far as the overall survey results are concerned, no single area or store dominated the data.

Differences—by Books Needed for Redemption. The spread of values was also examined in the light of the "book cost" or the number of books required to redeem. An array of books required with their corresponding class-average values reveals that the top benefits appear to lie with the lower costs in books required. The following table summarizes the results.

This outcome is not surprising. The Company's average redemption is two and one-quarter books. Since this mean is close to the absolute limit of zero compared with the single redemption that can require hundreds of books, the redemptions must form a highly skewed distribution. The median and the mode would therefore be something less than two and on-quarter books. In other words, the company's biggest volume lies in the first class—less than two books—followed

Table 19

SAMPLE VALUE PER BOOK BY BOOKS NEEDED FOR REDEMPTION

Books Required	Items in Sample	Value Per Book
Less than 2	32	$3.60
2 to 2¾	21	3.43
3 to 3¾	22	3.02
4 to 4¾	12	3.32
5 to 5¾	9	3.01
6 to 7¾	10	3.17
8 to 9¾	11	3.04
10 or More	12	2.80
Total	129	Average $3.25

by the "two to two and three-quarter" books class, and those are the quotation classes in which it can give the highest worth.

Differences — Economic Significance. Thus the dispersion was analyzed by merchandise category, cash-market pricing policy and availability, store type, city, and stamp-catalog quotation. In view of these price differences among items, the stability of the stratum means is reassuring — it corroborates the reliability of the $3.25 estimate per book.

It is hard to say what the redemption pattern would be if the pricing policy in the stamp channel reflected such differentials as transportation cost among cities and product margin among categories. Certainly the stamp channel would not be such an easy target for attack because of obvious low-value premiums that are a part of its line. Table 17 shows a remarkable consistency of stratum means. If many savers acted on a purchasing-power comparison between United States greenbacks and S & H Green Stamps, the stratum means in the table would fall into a pattern of descending values. The largest number of books would be tendered for the good values, and the mass of items with low redemptions would be of the type for which the monetary market has a comparative or even absolute advantage. Evidently, the public does not generally equate stamps with money or it just is not price-conscious on infrequently acquired merchandise. Since the saving cycle is long and the catalog handy, it must be concluded that the saver certainly does have an opportunity for comparison.

Post-Survey Evaluation

A post-evaluation of the sampling shows the degree to which the objectives in the survey design were met. The intent was (1) to protect the operation from direction by anyone with a stake in the results, and (2) to assure the representativeness of the sample and the responses.

The items were selected randomly in accordance with statistical methodology. Thus, no person influenced the selection. The writer sought to make the prices representative of the conventional market by specifying large stores, but the actual choice of cities was left to the research organization's president; the choice of retailers to the shoppers' supervisors. Again, no party at interest affected the type of response.

The Distribution of Sample Items. The distribution of the items actually included in the sample was compared with that of S & H redemption patterns. The sample followed fairly closely total redemptions — for example, the first 10% of the items in the sample represented 27% of redemptions while the Company's data showed that as few as 7% of the offerings accounted for 27% of the estimated redemptions. The sample was also compared to the population on the basis of book prices of items redeemed. The items in the sample and the responses were not so skewed as the Company data, that is to say the operation was relatively more successful in locating the more valuable (in terms of number of books required for redemption) items. The data in Table IV suggest that this may have biased the result downward. In other words, if a similar proportion of goods had been located in each cost range, the final estimate of the value per book might have been slightly higher.

The Problem of Unlocated Items. Another facet of the study that was given post-survey scrutiny was the 64.5% response rate and the problem of unlocated items. There were several possible reasons why they could not be found. Models in a manufacturer's line may change while articles carried in a trading stamp catalog must remain the same for the life of the catalog. Thus they may be available at redemption centers but obsolete at the retail level. Cards were returned from the field with the notation, "no longer carry this number/this model." Also some sample items were clearly out of season during mid-summer when the survey was conducted—a snow suit, for example—which meant they could not be located or priced. Some of the brands or items were not carried by the stores visited. There were also the inevitable few items which were "out of stock" or "on order."

Thus when the sample and the responses were compared to the universe, the agreement was good. Except for the possible under-representation of the low book-cost items there were no other indications that the items not located might 'have a larger or smaller value per book than those that were priced. This, together with a finding by The Sperry and Hutchinson Company that the average relationship between cost and *Ideabook*-quotation on the found articles was not significantly different from those not found, supported the conclusion that the 129 items were a fair and representative sample.

Summary of Overall Results. The combined experience of all these studies can be used to predict the outcome of any future research on this subject. As long as The Sperry & Hutchinson Company and the cash-market retailers maintain their separate merchandising and pricing policies the value of merchandise received per book of stamps will have a wide dispersion. Accordingly, a sample of stamp-book values is very likely to exceed the Company's sales proceeds for its stamps if

a) the sample is representative of redemptions
b) the response rate is high
c) the criterion is the retail market elected by many consumers (i.e., stores doing a large volume in manufacturers' branded goods)
d) the scope of the survey is consistent with the stamp company's area of operations

Conversely, the record clearly shows that an estimate of stamp-book value will quite likely fall below the company's realization if

a) a "non-probability" sample is dominated by small appliances or by high-cost listings (i.e., requiring many books to redeem)
b) the number of items priced is small
c) the criterion is a price that is rarely or never available to consumers (e.g., wholesale prices; close-outs or other temporary reductions; mail-order catalog prices excluding transportation cost, which are below the store prices of the same seller, etc.)
d) the scope of the test does not reflect the stamp company's area of operations.

By the same token, a small group comprised of say, hollowware and miscellaneous gifts or goods valued at manufacturers' suggested list prices is likely to give an unrealistically high estimate. However, no distortion in that direction was found in the literature screened.

The results of the present survey show that a saver of S & H Green Stamps is likely to obtain a higher value on most of the Company's line than the contracting retailer's first cost of the stamps. No attempt was made to quantify any indirect costs or benefits of the dealer and any indirect costs or benefits of the consumer. Nor was the degree of consumer satisfaction with service in redemption centers and conventional stores ascertained. In this survey a probability sample of redemption merchandisee was priced in large stores in six cities for the purpose of comparing the average retail value per book with the stamp company's average realization. The conclusion that the former exceeds the latter is statistically significant.

CHAPTER XI

TRADING STAMPS AND RETAIL PRICES

Probably no other facet of the stamp phenomenon has stirred interest as much as the claims and counterclaims of the impact on retail prices. "Who actually bears the cost of trading stamps concerns all of us," remarked a publication of the United States Department of Agriculture. "This question is one of the most controversial issues in the history of food retailing." [1]

In October 1966 thousands of housewives across the country protested against high food prices and many pointed to the supermarkets' promotional devices as an obvious cause. But the effect of stamps on retail prices is more elusive, and their effects on prices generally more subtle, than appears at first glance. Economic theory cannot readily predict the impact on the price level. Empirical research has been similarly inconclusive. At the micro level the incidence of cost is not uniform, and in the aggregate it cannot be traced. When one reflects that prominent economists disagree, for example, about who bears the burden of corporate income taxes, the inability to pinpoint the relatively tiny cost of stamps is not surprising. To give an inkling of but a few ramifications, the diffusion of stamp cost throughout the economy will be suggested at the end of this chapter.

What is Involved? It is not necessary to list all the complications to convey the frustrations of seeking a needle in a haystack. During the period of the supermarket-based stamp boom a general upcreep of prices occurred but the Consumer Price Index shows that retail food prices increased at a lesser rate than total prices. It also registered much sharper increases in the periods just before than since the mass conversions to the little tokens. After stamp usage declined, the pace of inflation quickened. It would be just as unprovable to say that the upward thrust in prices was checked by trading stamps as that they supported it.

A more direct inference can be made from the fact that prices have kept rising all along whereas a store's new cost after it uses stamps occurs only once. In fact, as noted in Table 5 of Chapter VI, the unit cost of stamps has been declining so that the average retailer using stamps in the late 1960's paid less than one using them in the 1950's. A usage of stamps certainly could not cause new increases in costs year after year, since all the cost is incurred in the first year.

There is a very simple way to quantify the upper limit on shifting the cost of stamps to the average consumer. Roughly, if a food store's cost is say, 2% of sales, and if in 1967 stamps were tied in with about 40% of all grocery volume, the overall burden works out to a total of 0.8% on all grocery sales. This average of less than a penny per dollar makes no allowance for the value of the premiums. It represents the merchants' cost; it does not take into account fractions that they may superimpose or absorb. The merchants could, for example, pass forward a little at a time — before, during, and after a conversion to stamps — but during more than 1½ decades the *total* effect of the increase has always been at most that penny per dollar, and not a *series* of increases as the American economy has been experiencing from other causes.

However, those who have researched this topic have found it much more complicated than this overview suggests. For example, when the United States Department of Agriculture published a study of comparative price changes about a decade ago, it noted that in 13 cities with 59% of the stores covered by the study, prices in stamp-giving stores increased more than average and in 8 cities with 41% coverage, prices in the stores that added stamps declined in relation to those of their nonstamp competitors. "Such variations may help to account for the many differences of opinion with regard to the overall impact of the use of stamps on food prices." [2]

The researchers also concluded that "the difference in price trends observed in this study may have been caused in part by nonstamp stores lowering food prices to meet the competition of stores adding trading stamps." [3] In contrast, one person suggested to this writer that the cost of stamps shifted to consumers by some stores may not affect stamp stores in particular but may instead act as an umbrella over all retailers so that empirical findings of no price differences mask the possibility that the minority of stamp users have enabled all stores to raise prices. This is what makes this question so fascinating; it is a fertile topic for speculation. No matter how far-fetched, conjectures cannot encompass the diversity of tactics in the market place. For example, a trade publication reported (disapprovingly) a merchant's decision to eliminate stamps and raise prices — an attempt to profit from consumers' expectation that he would do the opposite.

But imaginative enterprise is not the sole determinant. Policies must take into account consumers' responsiveness and competitors' retaliation. Instead of recouping any particular expense, marketing strategy tries to secure a satisfactory return on investment from a successful combination of tangible and intangible offerings; the range of discretion on price is probably smaller than on most other variables. Since a yes-no decision on stamps is inseparable from assumptions about volume, advertising, and other marketing variables, the executive of a large organization can only estimate the true cost-price connection. Some merchants who discontinued stamps were surprised how small a reduction in margin they achieved.[4]

Many spokesmen for gasoline retailers have complained that the operators cannot pass the cost forward. Statements from food chain executives have run the gamut: "We have had to increase prices because we give stamps" to "we would have to increase prices if stamps were discontinued." A cynic might say that those absorbing the cost have the greatest interest in claiming that it burdens the consumer, But a more plausible interpretation is that although a supermarket organization's cost-price relationship is indirect, the actual result of a conversion to or a defection from stamps does indeed differ from case to case.

The technical problems of tracing the impact of stamps seem to be unsurmountable. No two stores are alike; at the minimum their occupancy expense varies. As noted, pricing actions may be stamp-related yet they need not coincide with a store's stamp-policy change or they may occur because of somebody else's stamp-policy change. Prices vary at one point in time among stores and over a period of time in the same store — most often for reasons unrelated to stamps. In supermarkets, especially, the price of an article may even vary at one point in time at the same store because of the profusion of special deals and confusion due to frequent price changes. At the methodological level, there are problems of sampling and sample design.

Empirical Evidence. Nevertheless, many researchers have tried to isolate the link between trading stamps and retail prices. The studies reflect varying degrees of sophistication; some offer carefully documented interpretations of controlled research. To give a flavor of the evidence, a few examples of published information will be cited without delving too deeply into the statistical technicalities.

Verne A. Bunn, Associate Professor of Business Administration at

Wichita State University and later at the Midwest Research Institute devoted thirty months during 1960 to 1962 to a survey of food prices in an area with stamps and an adjacent area without trading stamps. The study checked the total price of a market basket which contained national brands wherever possible and standard grades where particular brands were not significant. Pricing was always done on the same day of the week, in a sample of stores which included each city's leading supermarkets and, where available, members of the same chain in neighboring stamp and nonstamp areas. Professor Bunn concluded that his studies reveal no evidence that the use of trading stamps, even on a widespread basis, leads to higher retail food prices. "In fact, the price level in the cities where stamps were in use was, in every case, actually a tiny bit lower than in the similar cities of neighboring states where stamps were banned or restricted."[5] A follow-up study in 1965 brought similar results: "On the average, stamp stores had prices 0.24% lower than non-stamp stores. This is particularly noticeable in comparing prices within a chain or affiliated group."[6]

In the previously discussed study by the United States Department of Agriculture, the researchers found an edge of six-tenths of one percent in terms of price trends in favor of the non-stamp stores.[7]

On the other hand, a substantial price differential emerged from the "unorthodox method"[8] employed by Professors James D. Bromley and William H. Wallace when they found an average increase in price of 2.02% in a study of one store. Finding that the store's "prices immediately before the stamps and immediately after the stamps were introduced were no different," the researchers then compared post-adoption prices with advertisements some three months before when "the case study store had encountered some serious competition . . ."[9] According to Professor Milton Alexander, who wrote a critique of the Bromley-Wallace study, "the shelf price [with stamps] test was conducted at a supermarket of a large chain in Wakefield, a semi-rural town in Rhode Island, while the advertised prices [without stamps] were for stores in the city of Providence, Rhode Island, some thirty miles away."[10] Professor Alexander, who is a member of the President's Panel on Consumer Education for People with Limited Income, made many additional criticisms of the Bromley-Wallace work. He pointed out that, among other things, due to arithmetical errors alone the Bromley-Wallace figure of 2.02% was 20% too low in one part of the study while elsewhere inaccurate arithmetic produced even more substantial errors.[11]

Thus, although it seems to be very difficult to establish the precise effect of trading stamps on retail prices, the major studies point to minimal differences between stamp and nonstamp stores on an overall basis. Comparisons with discount food stores might show greater differences, but it should be noted that stamp usage is not uncommon among discount outlets. Hence, absence of stamps is not specifically the cause of such price differentials.

In addition to possible sampling errors there is a source of difficulty which stems from the professional researcher's ignorance of the intangibles of the trade. Despite impeccable mathematical and technical credentials an investigator may encounter pitfalls in the peculiarities of the industry. A cognizant insider's survey is of special interest then. Such a survey was reported by William Golub, President of Central Markets, Inc., of Schenectady, before the State Conference on Store Trading Stamps conducted by Persia Campbell, then Consumer Counsel to the Governor of New York, on October 2, 1956.[12] An extract from Mr. Golub's testimony follows:

"I asked my men to go out to our major competitors in Schenectady and Albany, all that they could cover, and get as large a list of identical, advertised items carried by all stores as they could, with their prices, and let me see what the comparison was.

"The list is made up of nationally known and nationally advertised items in our staple grocery department. There are no items 'almost the same.' Sugar, flour—Gold Medal, Pillsbury, canned milk—Borden's, Pet, Betty Crocker products, tea—Tenderleaf, Tetley, Chef Boyardee, dog foods of all kinds, Beechnut products, Campbell's products, General Foods' products, all kinds of soaps, cereals—all articles identical with each other in size and amount. Seven stores were covered, namely our own, the A. & P., Loblaw's, Grand Union, Empire Markets, Grand Cash Markets and the Suburban Market in Schenectady. Four of these organizations issue stamps—Central Market, Loblaw, Grand Union, and Empire, while the A. & P., Grand Cash, and Suburban are not stamp users. And we found 139 identical items—you can multiply that because we did not, e.g. take fifty different baby foods and list as fifty but we listed them as one, and so on for other items; of these 139 items, these are the exact results as of yesterday, a Monday, when there are no prices varying because of specials, and this is the honest truth, verified by the signatures of these men. Central Markets total $54.26, A & P. total $54.31, Loblaw's total $54.79, Grand Union total $54.45, Empire, $54.67, Grand Cash —$54.51, and Suburban—$54.61. On the average, there is less than one-half per cent difference between all these organizations, and certain stamp issuing stores are as low or lower than their non-stamp issuing competitors. Where are your stamp costs being passed on to your consumers?

"We went further. We took a larger number of items which both our store and A. & P. carry, about 240 classifications, say 20 to 25 per cent of our staples, a mighty big cross-section and we came out within two cents in total costs—$97.63 in our store and $97.65 in A. & P.

"Those are the facts, gentlemen, they are not theory, they are not generalities. As I said, we did not know what the results would be when we went out on the survey. The costs of stamps are not being passed on to the consumer, they are an extra dividend, the result of competition, as are other advances which have been brought into our food line to the benefit of the consumer.

". . . When I said our survey covered 139 items, I should have explained that we started with about 300 categories. But in checking seven different organizations, we found that one did not carry certain items, or others were out of them so we brought the total down to 139 categories which were carried by all seven and all seven had in stock. These 139 items, however, do not represent just that number of items. They represent many more because, as I said earlier, baby foods, for instance, which may number forty or fifty were included as one, and so on. Now, we were able to make a more complete comparison between our prices and those at the A. & P. when we compared just the two organizations in approximately 240 price classifications (approximately 500-600 items), nationally advertised and identical in all cases, which represented easily 20 or 25 per cent of our total items and possibly 40 or 50 per cent of our dollar volume in staple groceries."

Mr. Golub's conclusions were challenged, as have been many other survey conclusions, on the basis of the representativeness of the sample. Only 139 categories in seven supermarkets and 240 price classifications in two markets were priced out of all that were handled. It was claimed that stamp-giving stores might have hidden price increases among slower-moving items. To cover a 2% over-all price rise in only a portion of a store's volume would imply some policy such as the following:

Assumed Per Cent of Dollar Volume to which Increases are Applied	Estimated Percentage Share of Items	Average Price Increase Needed on Selected Items to Effect an Overall 2% Rise
20%	34%	10%
10%	20%	20%
5%	10%	40%

This table shows that about one-third of a store's offerings would have to be raised 10% in order to accomplish a 2% overall price increase. A 10% price rise on that many items (about 1,700 then; more now) is certainly not insignificant. Alternatively, some five hundred articles would have to be increased an average of 40% to "hide" the cost of stamps. The accusations from competitors that the stamp-giving store is more expensive is likely to make the housewife more price-conscious, and further increase the risk of alienating her if prices rise. It appears to be difficult to conceal among the slow-moving items a price increase sufficient to compensate for the direct cost of stamps. To credit such a stratagem with success the opponents of trading stamps impute to the shopper an enormous range and domain of price insensitivity. If the consumer is that bland about prices, why had they not been marked up by everybody?

Does the average stamp-disbursing merchant have superior insights over the nonstamp retailer as regards the 5,000 or more revenue curves that face the supermarket operators daily? "Entrepreneurs are extremely vague in their ideas about demand curves," says R. F. Harrod.[13] Hence it is not surprising that the results of a survey conducted by the U. S. Department of Agriculture soon after the New York Hearings "do not substantiate the hypothesis that stamp stores charge higher prices for foods not regularly purchased by housewives."[14] What is surprising, however, is that such an hypothesis was advanced —and that an economist once even published it.[15]

Although purists may quarrel with Mr. Golub's pragmatic approach, it must be conceded that neither the locale nor the timing of his spot check was selected to obtain a particular result. Furthermore, the list of objectively comparable items used as a basis for the price test has no apparent bias relative to trading stamps.

Stamps aside, the price uniformity reported by Mr. Golub is striking. The finding is consistent with an assumption that in a given market area, retail prices might not be identical but that the differences will tend to be offsetting. This assumption was confirmed in 1966 by the staff of the National Commission on Food Marketing. "Given complete price information, the help of computers and all the clerical help needed, it is impossible to say which retailer in a particular community has lower prices," the staff found.[16]

Most studies of stamps and prices have centered in the food area. There has been little questioning of the impact of stamps on prices in other product lines. Studies by Benson & Benson, Inc., in July 1965 indicate that no price differential existed for gasoline at that time. They also researched drug store items and found that, again, there was no systematic differential between stamp-giving and nonstamp establishments.

Theoretical Analysis. In the realm of microeconomics, some of the diagnoses of actual behavior in the retail market are the theories of monopolistic competition, imperfect competition, oligopoly, and others. A detailed exposition of their relevance to trading stamps fits best into a separate volume. There has been very little effort to analyze trading stamps theoretically; a search of the literature elicited only two articles.[17] The authors of both studies pointed out that after a firm adopts stamps, the new equilibrium may theoretically be at a higher, the same, or at a lower price. By borrowing assumptions from economic theory that had been developed with other situations in mind, they both concluded that trading stamps are likely to increase prices.

These two contributions to the cost-price debate are mentioned only for the sake of comprehensiveness. By recourse to more realistic formulations, the analyses could have led to a different conclusion. In terms of their own setting, both authors made the technical error of treating marginal cost (or marginal revenue) as the extra outlay (or extra sales) due to stamps. An economic analysis of stamps must grapple with the changes in total cost and in total sales that they induce; it must consider alternative costs; and it must take account of long-term consequences.

Conclusion on Price Studies. The problem of describing and attributing changes in cost and revenue is considerably complicated by the fact that the stamp is not an isolated phenomenon. It interacts with virtually every other input. A store's experiments may indicate that it could increase its sales by 10% if it stayed open in the evening. The extra costs of the temporal expansion may exceed the extra revenue. If the store added stamps, its daytime schedule may limit the sales increase to say, 8%. But if the store adopted a stamp and extended its hours to the evening, it might enjoy a sales increase of say, 50%. Under the circumstances, a businessman would probably not try to assess the interaction because he considers it operationally unimportant. Presumably, data on experience with night openings would reflect the entire 50% gain; data on stamps would credit the entire gain to them. To the store owner the question is not how much the stamps cost and whether his customers will pay for them, but what is the end result of all the interrelated changes?

Over the years, managerial decisions and market pressures have varied. So has consumer responsiveness to stamps. In America the market is always in motion. The diverse results of the numerous empirical investigations reflect these continuous changes and, also, the differences in researchers' technical competence. As regards the cited theoretical investigations, it may be concluded that only a reasonable use of economic theory can lead to realistic results.

Toward a Theoretical Model of Stamps' Impact. The preceding discussion left indeterminate the question whether or not the saver pays for his stamps. A more detailed analysis is unlikely to yield a definitive answer although, of course, any solution can be forced by postulating nonexisting relationships. "Actually the economic life of a nonsocialist society consists of millions of relations or flows between individual firms and households. We can establish certain theorems about them, but we can never observe all of them."[18] In general, it may be asserted that the more that a cost exhibits certain characteristics the more difficult it will be to trace. These characeristics include:

> Small absolute amount per transaction
> Small relative amount per transaction
> Pervasiveness throughout the economy
> Uneven effects on the demand and supply sides
> Unstable effects on the demand and supply sides
> Discontinuous effects on the demand and supply sides
> Unknown complementary and substitutional relationships
> Possibility of hiding the impact
> Multicollinearity (common cause among economic variables)
> Two-way causation

The trading stamp has all of these characteristics. Retailing has chronic excess capacity which the stamp system may or may not relieve. Theory may still be serviceable in indicating the interrelationships and the probable causal patterns. In the interest of simplicity the value of premiums will be disregarded. Theoretically, in a market which is not governed solely by price an additional cost such as stamps is likely to be shifted forward to the saver if he manifests a low price elasticity of demand. The rational consumer then can either accept and pay for the stamps or shop at stores that do not use them. If the customers of stamp-givers do not really want stamps, ease of entry into retailing, the experimental spirit of the trade, closeness to the ultimate consumer, and aid from consumer-research technology will quickly cause the system to be abandoned. If a significant number of consumers accept stamps it will still be assumed that consumers' reactions are not uniform and that, in each market, stamp-featuring stores compete with merchants using other appeals. Obviously, if the consumer reimburses the merchant or if the consumer does not "buy" stamps there is no problem of assigning cost.

In the event that consumers refuse to reimburse the merchant for stamps but he uses them because he finds them effective, the cost incidence becomes more difficult to trace. The aggressive retailer will adopt stamps to draw trade away from competitors (case 1). Since the competitors cannot get the same franchise they, in turn, will adopt rival plans (case 2) or will successfully feature other appeals, especially to the stamp-resenting consumer segment (case 3). In cases 1 and 2, the cost of the stamp is absorbed by increased volume, lower profit, or reduced other expense. Included in the last instance is a backward shift of the cost. Co-existence of users and non-users (case 3) maximizes consumer choice, and consumer behavior determines cost incidence. If competitors cannot meet the stamp challenge they may suffer declines in volume leading to losses and eventual withdrawal from the market (case 4).

In general, most economic theories hypothesize that a reduction in the number of vendors, especially if it leads to inadequate facilities, will cause higher prices. But if the reduction merely eliminates some of the heretofore idle capacity, the survivors have at least the means of lowering prices—and would be forced to do so if the consumer is sufficiently price-conscious and the businessmen do not want to attract new rivals.

The decline and withdrawal conjectured for case 4 could be effectively offset by any of several forces: an overall expansion in demand for the services of all retailers, an increasing public apathy toward trading stamps, or the importance of these struggling outlets to their vendors. In the first instance the exclusivity of the trading stamp and the absence of monopoly profits among other retailers would keep out new retail entrants, thus enabling the marginal firm to recoup some volume losses from a generic expansion in demand. If the public is apathetic and shopping patterns do not shift due to stamps, the situation of the user (case 1) and his competitor who does not adopt stamps (case 4) will be reversed due not to the former's decline in volume but to his failure to expand and cover his added cost. Finally, if the supply function of the vendor to the marginal grocer is inelastic, the grocer can shift his losses backwards.

From the overview of the grocery trade as a whole, it can be seen that, to the extent that stamps either cause reductions among the number of retailers or hold down their increase when generic demand expands, the trade can offset stamp costs through greater absorption of fixed cost or other cost changes detailed elsewhere. There will be a net social gain if factors are retired that have alternative employments.

The economic variables involved in the cost of trading stamps can impinge in various ways upon the manufacturers as well as retailers. Vendors supplying stamp-using retailers would lose some volume if the promotional cost is passed through to the consumer, assuming the economy is static and demand elastic. Manufacturers in the aggregate would experience little effect from a redistribution of the volume at the retail level but a concentration of volume at some retailers would enable the manufacturers to achieve efficiencies in marketing and other activities. Again, a subsidy to keep marginal retailers in the market would be self-defeating in the aggregate but it may be economically rational for the individual competitor whose profit can be maximized by discrimination. It is also possible that, due to the type of articles involved or due to stamps, the demand for the tied goods is relatively inelastic, in which case the income effect of higher prices would fall against other, negatively cross-elastic, types of goods.

And to trace these effects to an even more general level, all along the way one will find some firms with expanding and others with declining profits. This will cause income-tax effects which are most unlikely to be offsetting. If there were a profits fund so that the distribution is a zero-sum game, the progressive rate structure would cause a rise in total collections.

The effects of trading stamps also reach laterally into other retail areas. The convenience-goods and unsought-goods trades are the most frequent users of stamps. The gummed coupons, in turn, are usually redeemed for shopping and specialty goods. Theoretically, if the consumer pays for the stamps and collects a lower, equal, or higher value in redemption merchandise his real income has correspondingly decreased, remained the same, or increased. Aside from these effects on purchasing power, if the premium is a substitute for merchandise that the consumer would have bought, its purchase price is instead available to him in cash for other spending or investment. If the premium is a complement of other wares, its receipt is likely to stimulate purchases from retailers of shopping and specialty goods. In either event their trade is likely to expand due to stamps. Some retail transactions might be deferred, if the saver waits until he has accumulated the stamps, or accelerated, if the article to be acquired with stamps does not dominate the timing. And finally, if the premium is an independent article, that is, one that the consumer would not have bought in the cash market, there will be no effect on retailers of related merchandise. One can trace parallel effects for manufacturers of substitute, complementary, and independent wares.

Although these ramifications are not exhaustive, there seems to be no need to pursue other possible consequences. Instead, it may come as a refreshing change that there also have been accusations that trading stamps lower prices. Some of this evidence was introduced in cases before the courts and regulatory commissions, for example, which involved the controversy of whether a store's policy of giving stamps decreases a manufacturer's standard retail price. The legal findings have varied. Sumner Slichter reasoned that only extra stamps should be deemed a form of price reduction; "when, however, they are given in equal ratio on all articles they are not a form of price-cutting and the legal prohibitions applicable to price-cutting should not be extended to include the uniform and indiscriminate giving of stamps." [19]

The enactment of state resale price maintenance laws and the Miller-Tydings Act in the 1930's added new fuel to the dispute. Indeed, just before the supermarket-based stamp popularity of the 1950's began, a well-known economist concluded that ". . . the trading stamp is primarily the product of resale price maintenance. If this source of market imperfection were removed, most of this form of trading would disappear." [20] It appears that this statement was neither accurate history nor sound prediction. The supermarket is certainly one of the least likely places involved in resale price maintenance.

Throughout the economy, obviously, the repercussions to stamps are many and varied. The tortuous path depicted above is neither complete nor quantifiable. It suggests that a model that realistically monitors the impact of trading stamps on prices, if one can be constructed, will be more complex than a glib assertion that stamps have some particular effect on retail prices.

Summary. The analyst who seeks to trace the cost of trading stamps must compare slopes of revenue curves with slopes of cost curves. The initial comparison will encompass revenue versus cost slopes of the goods or services on which stamps are given; then the comparison must be extended to the slopes of all other products.

In the beginning the cost impact will fall mainly on the contracting retailer, and he will seek to absorb it out of increased volume on the same fixed cost base. The burden will remain with the retailer if his customers' demand and his vendors' supply are elastic. Some retailers will let the cost of stamps encroach on their profits. This implies that this cost had formerly been an economic rent. The reduction in this surplus over the minimum incentive needed (really their alternative opportunities) will be partially offset through lower taxes. Here as elsewhere the cost incidence will eventually be diffused.

Competitors without stamps may try to gain volume by lowering prices, provided consumers are cost-conscious. If the total demand does not expand, the concentration of patronage will make some stores extra-marginal. To the extent that the retired resources have alternative uses there will be a net social gain. With the same volume as before handled through fewer stores, at the same prices plus stamps or at lower prices, the resulting efficiency gives rise to a consumer surplus.

Thus in the long run there will be a new equilibrium of which stamps are an insignificant albeit integral part. If they are then discontinued, a reversion to the previous equilibrium is an improbable accident. The gains and losses due to a cessation of the system would flow according to the relative inelasticities. Most likely, in the absence of stamps there would be an immediate scramble for a substitute promotional device. (Studies show that this occurred in Kansas where stamps are illegal.)

But if the consumer prefers the convenience of more stores and also wants stamps, his demand will be inelastic and the cost of both will gravitate toward him. Conversely the costs of stamps and stores would fall on the vendors or factors whose supply is inelastic. The lower the elasticity of the consumer's demand or the vendor's supply, the greater the likelihood of cost incidence.

If the burden falls on the consumer in the form of higher prices, he must decide whether he wants to substitute purchases in the stamp market for purchases in the conventional market. The effects will be distributed in accordance with the reactions to his choices. His decisions will have an aggregate impact insofar as the two channels differ in production functions and efficiency.

On the other hand, the vendor with an inelastic supply will absorb the cost, subject to diffusion through lower taxes, as long as he has no alternative uses for his facilities. In the long run, equipment will wear out, substitutes will become available, population and purchasing power may grow, so that all supply and demand will tend to become more elastic.

Chapter XII

TRADING STAMPS IN ECONOMIC PERSPECTIVE

Trading stamps perform certain economic functions, entail economic costs, and confer economic benefits. What is the system's economic significance to consumers, retailers, stamp companies, and the total economy? From the examination of these points a number of conclusions have emerged.

Summary of Findings

1. Trading stamps seem obvious and simple but they reflect an inextricable conglomeration of consumer motivations and market dynamics. Their serviceability has been as diverse as the personalities of people and the conditions of commerce. Taking an economic point of vantage, the writer concludes that trading stamps are neither categorically good nor categorically bad. But interpretations will differ. The reader is invited to pass judgment on the evidence presented.

2. Trading stamps may be viewed analytically as having two major economic functions: to alleviate destructive competition among retailers of convenience goods and to facilitate consumption of wanted but dispensable merchandise among savers. More realistically, trading stamps are a promotional service for some retailers and manufacturers plus an incentive plan for employers. From the consumer's point of view, they are a fractional merchandise certificate.

3. Trading stamps have passed through three separate phases since the 1890's: popularity—apathy—poularity. They have flourished when they were needed as a distinguishing and ingratiating medium by firms having repetitive transactions with the public and when the latter was in a sufficiently receptive frame of mind to make them effective. They were at the height of their popularity in the middle 1960's; since then their usage in the retail sector has decreased slightly.

4. Trading stamps can yield an excellent return on investment for a small number of highly efficient stamp companies which have enjoyed spectacular growth since the 1950's. In the late 1960's these oligopolists are under heavy pressure by intra-industry rivalry, legal-legislative attacks, and defections of customers.

5. Trading stamps are a minor element in the total United States economy. In 1967 a small decline in stamp volume placed sales of the entire industry at approximately 750 million dollars. Although a stamp may be important to the retailers, merchandise suppliers, employees, or localities where its impact is concentrated, when the results diffuse throughout the general economy, even considering any possible multiplier effect, they are so small as to become untraceable.

6. Trading stamps also are of very modest value to the individual consumer. What, then, explains the quasi-currency's popularity? It appears that for most savers the stamp is the means to satisfactions that would be unfulfilled without it. Some further implications will be discussed below. The small minority of consumers who throw it away or lose it is making a transfer payment (not necessarily at explicit cost) to the system. Within limits, the abstentions can be very helpful to the participants.

7. Trading stamps may or may not affect retail prices. Realistic formulations of economic theory do not support a prediction of a price change in one direction to the exclusion of one in the opposite direction, and the results of empirical tests are similarly inconclusive. If the consumer is price-conscious and stamps are regarded as a gift, economic theory would predict that prices for a basket of frequently bought goods in one market area would tend toward equality among the competing merchants regardless of their stamp policies.

8. Trading stamps of one company tested provide redemption merchandise of higher average retail value than that company's average proceeds from the stamps it issues. In this sense, savers can benefit even if the retailer's cost is passed on to them, but there are wide dispersions about both averages.

9. Trading stamps may win popularity contests among women but not among retail merchants. The service is an expense to retailers which they incur as long as they believe that the stamp's various effects will at least offset its cost (or that lack of stamps would result in an opportunity loss). The effectiveness of the medium varies substantially, even between settings that are superficially similar. This variety of experience by merchants, in value to consumers, and in impact on prices is a sufficient reason for contradictory findings on the subject.

These points are not exhaustive, of course, and the preceding chapters present many other findings together with their documentation. In the first chapter it was brought out that the stamp system has a cultural aspect that may serve as an additional basis for interpretation. A strictly economic perspective cannot be complete but it may sharpen insights and promote understanding.

SOMETHING INSTEAD OF NOTHING

An attempt to theorize why trading stamps have become a household word—and chore—in the past one and a half decades must look to their unique characteristic. It is, in the view of the writer, their power to command goods with a high personal priority but for which a money outlay is institutionally proscribed. In other words, if the consumer had the equivalent amount of cash instead of stamps, she would not often purchase the merchandise that is redeemed with them because social or cultural conventions would dictate other allocations. Thus the non-liquidity feature, the restriction to redemption merchandise, may produce a "super-rational" reaction from some savers — a preference for stamps over paltry amounts of money and fleeting moments of time. There are, of course, many other variables; different people have different reasons.

Most savers probably do not realize that, in the aggregate, no choice of stamps versus equivalent amounts of cash exists. When stamps are discontinued, the semi-price competition is likely to be replaced by non-price competition or simply by more competitors, not by lasting price reductions. Further, the savers may not have realized that the retail value of the goods redeemed is, on average, some 21% higher than the average amount paid by users, if S & H is typical. This extra subsidy is made possible by the unredeemed stamps, the income on outstanding stamps, and the efficiency of moving a concentrated variety of goods in large and predictable volume from manufacturers to redemption centers. Perhaps some savers reason that because of living patterns the alternative to stamps is doing without the goods received through them and that because of shopping patterns no cash savings are likely to take the place of stamps. Furthermore, even if the retailer's average cost were paid out to consumers, they would still lose the additional 21%. If the stamp savers sense these economic implications, their behavior may be appropriately described not as super-rational but as rational.

REFERENCES

CHAPTER I

1. Peter Longworth, "Trading Gets the Stamp of Respectability," *Evening Post* (Great Britain) (August 9, 1965), p. 5.

2. Harvey L. Vredenburg, *Trading Stamps* (Bloomington, Indiana: Bureau of Business Research, School of Business, Indiana University, 1956) and Christina Fulop, *The Role of Trading Stamps in Retail Competition* (London, England: Institute of Economic Affairs Limited, 1964).

3. Brian J. Strum, "Trading Stamps," *New York University Law Review*, Vol. 37, p. 1126.

4. Massachusetts Legislative Research Council, *Report Relative to Trading Stamps*, Senate No. 912, (April 28, 1964), p. 18.

5. U. S. Department of Agriculture, "Trading Stamps and Their Impact on Food Prices," (Washington, D. C.: U. S. Government Printing Office, 1958, p. 1.

U. S. Department of Agriculture, "Do Trading Stamps Affect Food Costs?" (Washington, D. C.: U. S. Government Printing Office, 1957), p. 4.

"Truth in Trading Stamps," statement prepared for delivery by Congressman Lester L. Wolff before the House Committee on Interstate and Foreign Commerce, August 17, 1966.

8. John Stuart Mill, *Principles of Political Economy*, Book II, Chapter IV, Section 3, cited approvingly in Edward H. Chamberlin, *The Theory of Monopolistic Competition*, 8th ed. (Cambridge, Mass.: Harvard University Press, 1965), p. 109.

9. Marcel Mauss, *The Gift*, translated by Jan Cunnison (Glencoe, Ill.: *The Free Press*, 1954), p. 1.

10. *Ibid., p.* 70.   11. *Ibid.,* p. 71.

CHAPTER II

1. Milton Friedman and Anna Jacobson Schwartz, *A Monetary History of the United States 1867-1960,* National Bureau of Economic Research, Studies in Business Cycles, No. 12 (Princeton, N. J.: Princeton University Press, 1963), p. 650.

2. Rance d/b/a Trading Stamp Exchange v. The Sperry and Hutchinson Co., 410 P. 2d 859 (1965) cert. to U. S. Supreme Court denied 382 U.S. 945 (1965).

3. "Glue on Our Tongues," *Consumer Reports* (October, 1962), p. 515.

4. Richard L. D. Morse, "Trading Stamps—A Consumer's View" (Manhattan, Kansas: Department of Family Economics, Kansas State University, 1965), p. 20.

5. Otto A. Davis, "The Economics of Trading Stamps," *The Journal of Business* (April, 1959), p. 148.

6. "Consumers Still Like Trading Stamps,' *Supermarket Merchandising* (July, 1961). Article on survey, "A Study on Trading Stamp Saturation" by Dr. Bertrand Klass.

7. Curt Kornblau, "The Super Market Industry Speaks" (Chicago, Ill.: The Institute).

CHAPTER III

1. Alfred W. Stonier and Douglas C. Hague, A Textbook of Economic Theory, 2nd ed. (London: Longmans, Green and Company, Ltd., 1957), p. 42.

2. 360 U.S. 334.

3. National Commission on Food Marketing, Organization and Competition in Food Retailing. Technical Study No. 7. (Washington, D. C.: U. S. Government Printing Office, 1966), p. 175.

4. Profit Parade (December, 1964).

5. Albert Haring and Wallace O. Yoder, eds., Trading Stamp Practice and Pricing Policy (Bloomington, Indiana: Bureau of Business Research, School of Business, Indiana University, 1958), p. 64.

6. J. S. Duesenberry, Income, Saving, and the Theory of Consumer Behavior (Cambridge, Mass.: Harvard Press, 1949), p. 28.

7. Ruth P. Mack, "Trends in American Consumption and the Aspiration to Consume," American Economic Review (May, 1956).

8. Sumner H. Slichter, Report on Coupons, Trading Stamps and Premium Systems (New York: Alexander Hamilton Institute, Report No. 68, 1916), p. 29.

9. Albert Haring, "Promoting Sales Through Merchandise Incentives" (Speech before Trading Stamp Institute, Atlantic City, July 14, 1960), p. 5.

10. George Katona, The Powerful Consumer (New York: McGraw-Hill Book Co., Inc., 1960), p. 148.

11. Richard Hammer, "Will Trading Stamps Stick?" Fortune (August, 1960), p. 119.

12. "Are Trading Stamps Losing Their Punch?" "Business Week (September 4, 1965), p. 67.

13. H. S. Houthakker and Lester D. Taylor, Consumer Demand in the United States 1929-1970 (Cambridge, Mass.: Harvard University Press, 1966), p. 195.

14. Leverett S. Lyon with the assistance of Helen May Wheeler, The Economics of Free Deals (Washington, D. C.: The Brookings Institution, 1933), p. 153.

15. H. L. Grathwohl, Trading Stamps: Theory and Practice (Vermillion, S. D.: Business Research Bureau, School of Business, State University of South Dakota, 1958), p. 34.

16. U. S. Department of Agriculture, "Food Retailing by Discount Houses" (Washington, D. C.: U. S. Government Printing Office, 1967), p. 13.

17. Edmund P. Learned and Catherine C. Ellsworth, Gasoline Pricing in Ohio (Boston, Mass.: Division of Research, Graduate School of Business Administration, Harvard University, 1959), p. 172.

18. Harvey L. Vredenburg, Trading Stamps in the Service Station (Iowa City, Iowa: Bureau of Business and Economic Research, College of Business Administration, State University of Iowa, 1959), pp. 13, 27, 29.

19. "Stamps," National Petroleum News (June, 1958), p. 115.

20. Denver Post (Colorado) (September 6, 1966).

21. Alfred R. Oxenfeldt, Executive Action in Marketing (Belmont, Cal.: Wadsworth Publishing Co., Inc., 1966), p. 602.

22. Douglas Dalrymple, "The Effect of Trading Stamps on the Sale of Applesauce," Merchandising Experiments, Paper No. 2 (Ithica, N. Y.: Department of Agricultural Economics, Cornell University Agricultural Experimental Station,

New York State College of Agriculture, Unit of the State University of New York, Cornell University, October, 1958), p. 4.

23. *1963 Study of Supermarket Shoppers* (Cincinnati, Ohio: Burgoyne Index, Inc., 1963), p. 36.

24. See, for example, *Look Magazine*, National Survey of Super Market Shopping 1963, conducted by Universal Marketing Research, Inc., an affiliate of Alfred Politz Research, Inc., Section II, "Trading Stamps," p. 52, and Ben L. Schapker, "Behavior Patterns of Supermarket Shoppers," *Journal of Marketing*, Vol. 30 (October, 1966), p. 48.

25. Robert D. Brennan, "Trading Stamps as an Incentive in Mail Surveys," *Journal of Marketing*, Vol. 22, No. 3 (January, 1958), p. 306.

26. Kurt G. Voss, "Trading-Stamp Storm Keeps Momentum," *The Christian Science Monitor* (October 19, 1965), p. 14.

27. David A. Loehwing, "Counter Revolution?" *Barron's* (October 12, 1964), p. 3.

28. Don't Just Drop Stamps—Give Customers Something Better," *Progressive Grocer* (February, 1963), pp. 69-72.

29. "Korvette Indicated Net in Fourth Quarter Fell Sharply From Fiscal '64," *The Wall Street Journal* (September 6, 1965), p. 6.

30. Alfred R. Oxenfeldt, *op. cit.*, p. 602.

31. R. L. D. Morse, *op. cit.* in Chapter 2, p. 16.

32. Stuart U. Rich, *Shopping Behavior of Department Store Customers* (Boston, Mass.: Division of Research, Graduate School of Business Administration, Harvard University, 1963).

33. E. A. G. Robinson, *The Structure of Competitive Industry* (Cambridge, England: The University Press, and London, England: Nisbet and Company, Ltd., 1931), pp. 172-173.

34. Ruby Turner Norris, *The Theory of Consumer's Demand*, rev. ed., (New Haven, Conn.: Yale University Press, 1952), p. 70.

35. National Commission on Food Marketing, *Food from Farmer to Consumer* (Washington, D. C.: U. S. Government Printing Office, 1966), p. 98.

36. Bristol-Myers Company v. Lit Brothers, 336 Pa. 81, 91, 6 A 2d 843, 848 (1939).

CHAPTER IV

1. E. T. Grether, *Marketing and Public Policy* (Englewood Cliffs, N. J.: Prentice-Hall, Inc., 1966), pp. 23-24.

2. Malcolm P. McNair, "Significant Trends and Developments in the Postwar Period' (in A. B. Smith, ed., "Competitive Distribution in a Free, High-Level Economy and Its Implications for the University." Pittsburgh, Pa.: University of Pittsburgh Press, 1958).

3. D. L. Shawver, *The Development of Theories of Retail Price Determination* (Urbana, Ill.: University of Illinois Press, 1956), p. 92. See also Robert A. Triffin, *Monopolistic Competition and General Equilibrium Theory* (Cambridge, Mass.: Harvard University Press, 1940), Chapter V.

4. E. A. G. Robinson, *op. cit.* in Chapter 3, p. 118.

5. George J. Stigler, *The Theory of Price,* 3rd ed. New York: The Macmillan Company, 1966), p. 153.

6. E. A. G. Robinson, *op. cit.* in Chapter 3, p. 68.

7. Edith Tilton Penrose, *The Theory of the Growth of the Firm* (New York: John Wiley and Sons, Inc., 1959), p. 117.

8. Ralph Cassady, Jr., *Competition and Price Making in Food Retailing* (New York: The Ronald Press Co., 1962), pp. 73 ff.

9. C. Wright Mills, *White Collar, The American Middle Classes* (New York: Oxford University Press, 1951), p. 178.

10. H. Pasdermadjian, *The Department Store* (London, England: Newman Books, 1954), p. 29.

11. John W. Ferry, *History of the Department Store* (New York: The Macmillan Company, 1960), p. 94.

12. Leverett S. Lyon with the assistance of Helen May Wheeler, *op. cit.* in Chapter 3, p. 153.

13. Sumner Slichter, *op. cit.* in Chapter 3, pp. 7, 9. See also Ralph M. Hower, *History of Macy's of New York* (Cambridge, Mass.: Harvard University Press, 1943), pp. 268, 294; and John P. Nichols, *The Chain Store Tells Its Story* (New York: Institute of Distribution, Inc., 1940), p. 60.

14. Carl Menger, *Principles of Economics,* Translated and edited by James Dingwall and Bert F. Hoselitz (Glencoe, Ill.: The Free Press, 1950), p. 271.

15. L. S. Lyon with H. M. Wheeler, *op. cit.* in Chapter 3, pp. 32-33.

16. United States Department of Commerce, Bureau of Census, *1963 Census of Business* (Washington, D. C.: U. S. Government Printing Offiice, 1966).

17. Nichols, *op. cit.,* p. 60.

18. William S. Beinecke, "Save as You Spend: The Rise of Trading Stamps in Retail Promotion," (in: *Business Decisions That Changed Our Lives,* ed. by S. Furst and M. Sherman, New York: Random House, Inc., 1964), p. 341.

19. Slichter, *op. cit.* in Chapter 3, p. 3.

20. Joe S. Bain, *Industrial Organization* (New York: John Wiley and Sons, Inc., 1959), p. 441.

21. *Ibid.,* p. 444.

22. U. S. Department of Commerce, *1963 Census of Business, op. cit.*

23. Theodore N. Beckman and William R. Davidson, *Marketing,* 7th ed. (New York: The Ronald Press Co., 1962), p. 229.

24. Edward Chamberlin, *The Theory of Monopolistic Competition* (Cambridge, Mass.: Harvard University Press, 1935), pp. 105-106.

25. *Statistics of Income,* Source Books: Corporation Income Tax Returns, Internal Revenue Service, taken from National Commission on Food Marketing, *Organization and Competition in Food Retailing, op. cit.* in Chapter 3, p. 224.

26. Willard F. Mueller, "Trends in Gross Profit Margins of Food Retailers" (Washington, D. C.: Federal Trade Commission, May 5, 1965) Appendix, Table 2.

27. Eugene R. Beem, "Competitive Behavior and Trading Stamps in Food Retailing" (Testimony before the National Commission on Food Marketing, Washington, D. C., May 5-8, 1965), p. 10 and Exhibit 3.

28. McKinsey-General Foods Study, "The Economics of Food Distributors" (October, 1963), p. 8.

29. Richard Hammer, *op. cit.* in Chapter 3, p. 118.

30. George J. Church, "Give-away Selling Tool Draws New Grocer Ire, A Probe by the F.T.C.," *The Wall Street Journal* (April 13, 1956), p. 8.

31. "The Punch of the Stamps," *Business Week* (September 10, 1955), p. 28. See also, Hammer, *op. cit.* in Chapter 3, p. 213, and Mary McGee Williams, "You and the New Trading Stamp War," *Pageant* (December, 1962).

32. André Fontaine, "Trading Stamps—Who Gets What?" *Reader's Digest* (June, 1963), p. 69.

33. National Commission on Food Marketing, *Organization and Competition in Food Retailing, op. cit.,* p. 440.

43 .Curt Kornblau, "The Super Market Industry Speaks" (Chicago, Ill.: The Institute, annual).

35. J. J. Trout, "How Stamps Affect Volume and Earnings," *Progressive Grocer* (August, 1956).

36. Bertrand Klass, *Motivation and the Retail Food Business* (Palo Alto, Cal.: Stanford Research Institute, 1960).

37. *Look* Magazine, *National Survey of Super Market Shopping 1963, op. cit.* in Chapter 3, pp. 37 ff.

38. U. S. Department of Agriculture, "Do Trading Stamps Affect Food Costs?" *op. cit.* in Chapter 1, p. 6.

39. "Consumers Still Like Trading Stamps," *Super Market Merchandising, op. cit.* in Chapter 2.

40. Douglas J. Dalrymple, "The Effect of Trading Stamps on the Sale of Frozen Cherries," *Merchandising Experiments*, Paper No. 10, Department of Agricultural Economics, Cornell University Agricultural Experimental Station, New York State College of Agriculture, Cornell University, Ithica, N. Y., November, 1959.

41. Sumner H. Slichter, *op. cit.* in Chapter 3, p. 11.

42. Thomas J. Bray, "Just Fill in the Blank: Firms, Seeking Sales, Try Zany Sweepstakes," *The Wall Street Journal* (May 9, 1966), pp. 1, 10.

43. George Katona, *op. cit.* in Chapter 3, p. 238.

44. Lawrence W. Bell, "Stamps be Damned?" *Premium Practice* (June, 1965), p. 28.

45. George J. Stigler, *The Theory of Price,* op. cit., p. 199.

46. "Stamps be Damned," *Grocer Graphic* (May 3, 1965), pp. 12, 13.

47. "Safeway Says Sales in Second Period Run 12 Per Cent Ahead of Last Year," *The Wall Street Journal* (May 27, 1966).

48. James F. Bylin, "Safeway, Trail Blazer in Game Promotion, Will Drop All Games to Please Housewives," *The Wall Street Journal* (November 29, 1966), p. 5.

49. "Financial Reports Put Hex on Stamp-Droppers," *Premium Practice* (May, 1966), p. 74.

50. "What's Going On in Trading Stamps?" *Progressive Grocer* (February, 1965), p. 60.

51. "Trading Stamps Resumed by Massachusetts Chain," *The Wall Street Journal* (May 17, 1966).

52. "Stop and Shop Expects First Fiscal 16-Week Sales to Rise Sharply," *The Wall Street Journal* (September 22, 1965). See also "Korvette Loss Widened

in Fiscal Third Period; Coan Elected Chairman," *The Wall Street Journal* (May 28, 1965).

53. Willard W. Cochrane and Carolyn S. Bell, *The Economics of Consumption* (New York: McGraw-Hill Book Co., Inc., 1956), p. 373 (Italics in original).

54. Stanley C. Hollander, "The Wheel of Retailing," (in: *Marketing and the BehavioralSciences*, ed. Perry Bliss (Boston, Mass.: Allyn and Bacon, Inc., 1963), p. 319.

55. Eugene R. Beem and A. R. Oxenfeldt, "A Diversity Theory for Market Processes in Food Retailing," *Journal of Farm Economics*, (August, 1966), p. 80.

CHAPTER V

1. *National Petroleum News Year Book* (Mid-May, 1966), p. 138.

2. Simon N. Whitney, *Antitrust Policies: American Experience in Twenty Industries* (New York: Twentieth Century Fund, Inc., 1958), p. 157.

3. H. L. Vredenburg, *Trading Stamps in the Service Station, op. cit.* in Chapter 3, p. 22.

4. "Stamps," *National Petroleum News, op. cit.* in Chapter 3, p. 114.

5. Edmund P. Learned and Catherine C. Ellsworth, *op. cit.* in Chapter 3, p. 168.

6. New Jersey State Assembly, *Public Hearing before Special Assembly Committee to Study Trading Stamps and Similar Merchandising Devices* (Reconstituted under Assembly Resolution No. 2, 1963), Second Day, Jersey City, New Jersey, April 5, 1963, pp. 50, 40-A.

7. *Ibid.*, p. 19.   8. Bertrand Klass, *op. cit.* in ch. 4.

9. New Jersey State Assembly, *op. cit.*, p. 68-A.

10. *Ibid.*, pp. 77, 44-A.   11. *Ibid.*, pp. 70, 72, 73-A.

12. *Ibid.*, pp. 70, 36-A.   13. *Ibid.*, p. 1-A.

14. *Ibid.*, p. 54-A   15. *Ibid.*, p. 51-A.

16. George J. Stigler, *op. cit.* in Chapter 4, p. 184.

17. Walter Adams, *The Structure of American Industry*, 3rd ed. (New York: The Macmillan Co., 1961), p. 303.

18. Simon N. Whitney, *op. cit.*, p. 175.

19. Walter Adams, *op. cit.*, p. 303 fn.61.

20. *A Survey of Trading Stamp Savers*, Consumer Research Report IM-463 (Columbus, Indiana: Hamilton Cosco, Inc., 1963).

21. *Vide* Calvin J. Train, "The Inside Facts About Trading Stamps" (Annandale, Va.: J. & J. Publishing Co., Inc., 1964), pp.96-104.

CHAPTER VI

1. U. S. Department of Commerce, Bureau of Census, "Enterprise Statistics: 1963—Preliminary Report," ES63P-1, n. d. and letter from U. S. Department of Commerce, Bureau of the Census, dated November 8, 1965.

2. Massachusetts Legislative Research Council, *op. cit.* in Chapter 1, p. 49.

3. H. L. Grathwohl, *op. cit.* in Chapter 3, p. 51.

4. "Blue Chip Stamp Co. Consent Judgment Approved by Court,"*The Wall Street Journal* (June 7, 1967), p. 22.

5. "Allied Super Markets Sues Kroger Top Value on Trade Stamp Prices," *The Wall Street Journal* (June 29, 1966), p. 13.

6. "Analytical Report on Merchants Green Trading Stamp Co., Inc. (New York: Dun and Bradstreet, Inc., March 19, 1964).

7. Filed with the Office of the Secretary of State, Hartford, Conn.

8. Michigan Annual Report 1966 filed with the Michigan Corporation and Securities Commission, Lansing, Mich.

9. U. S. Department of Agriculture, "Trading Stamps and Their Impact on Food Prices," *op. cit.* in Chapter 1, p. 5.

10. National Commission on Food Marketing, *Organization and Competition in Food Retailing, op. cit.* in Chapter 3, p. 441.

11. "No. 1 California Stamp Company to Dissolve," *Business Week* (July 30, 1966), p. 36.

12. National Commission on Food Marketing, *op. cit.*, p. 441.

13. Advertisement of E. F. MacDonald Stamp Company in *The Wall Street Journal* (May 12, 1966), p. 15.

14. E. Wimmer, Jr. and Chad P. Wick, *The Truth About Trading Stamps* (Covington, Ky.: Forward America, Inc., n. d.), pp. 10, 11.

15. Unterberg and Unterberg, Counsel, before the United States Securities and Exchange Commission. In the matter of The Sperry and Hutchinson Company *et al* in behalf of Food Industry Alliance, Inc., p. 61.

CHAPTER VII

1. E. T. Grether, *op. cit.* in Chapter 4, p. 55.

2. U. S. Department of Agriculture, "Trading Stamps and Their Impact on Food Prices," *op. cit.* in Chapter 1, p. 10.

3. "Stamp Act 1962," *Television Age* (November 12, 1962), p. 34.

4. The Sperry and Hutchinson Company, "Preliminary Prospectus in the Offering of Common Stock" (April 20, 1966), p. 5.

5. "Stamp Act 1962," *Supra* Note 3.

6. *Look* Magazine, National Survey of Super Marketing Shopping 1963, *op. cit.* in Chapter 3, p. 48.

7. L. S. Lyon with the assistance of H. M. Wheeler, *op. cit.* in Chapter 3, p. 35.

8. For example, Action Discount Dollars Corporation, New York.

9. For example, Dilbert's Quality Supermarkets, Inc., Mineola, N. Y.

10. William S. Beinecke, *op. cit.* in Chapter 4, *passim.*

11. 378 U. S. 158.

12. Federal Trade Commission v. The Procter and Gamble Co.

13. "Everybody is an Expert on Inflation," *Business Week* (February 26, 1966), p. 174.

14. Jules Backman, *Advertising and Competition* (New York: New York University Press, 1967), p. v.

15. See, for example, Vance Packard, *The Waste Makers* (New York: Pocket Books, Inc., 1963), p. 123.

16. U. S. Department of Agriculture, "Trading Stamps and Their Impact on Food Prices," *op. cit.* in Chapter 1, p. 3.

17. *The Anti-stamper.* Story of the Trading Stamp Swindle. (New York: Anti-Stamper Association, 1904), p. 1.

CHAPTER VIII

1. William S. Beinecke, *op. cit.* in Chapter 4, p. 347.

2. George Meredith, *Effective Merchandising With Premiums* (New York: McGraw-Hill Book Co., Inc., 1962), p. 230.

3. E. T. Grether, "External Product and Enterprise Differentiation and Consumer Behavior" (in: *Consumer Behavior and Motivation*, ed. Robert H. Cole. Urbana, Ill.: University of Illinois, Bureau of Business Management, 1955), *passim.*

4. E. T. Grether, *Marketing and Public Policy, op cit.* in Chapter 4, p. 23.

5. John Michael, "The Billion-Dollar Industry Without an Accounting Textbook" (Prepublication manuscript, 1967).

6. National Commission on Food Marketing, *Organization and Competition in Food Retailing, op. cit.* in Chapter 3, p. 444.

7. Sources and notes for Table 12:
   a. Annual Report of The Sperry and Hutchinson Company, 1966.
   b. Includes accrued state and local taxes and payroll.
   c. Michigan Annual Reports, 1966, filed with the Michigan Corporation and Securities Commission, Lansing, Mich.
   d. *Supermarket News,* July 18, 1966, p. 1.
   e. Balance Sheets filed with Secretary of State, Hartford, Conn.
   f. Writer's estimates
   g. Includes accounts payable and accrued expenses
   h. Includes accrued federal income taxes.

8. Milton Friedman and Anna Jacobson Schwartz, *op. cit.* in Chapter 2, p. 443.

9. National Commission on Food Marketing, *Cost Components of Farm-Retail Price Spreads for Food.* (Washington, D. C.: U. S. Government Printing Office, 1966), p. 1.

10. Massachusetts Legislative Research Council, *op. cit.* in Chapter 1, p. 87.

11. *Ibid.,* p. 84.   12. *Ibid.,* p. 87.

13. Conrad Jameson, *Stamp Trading,* A Consumer Council study (London, England: Her Majesty's Stationery Office, 1964), p. 43.

14. "Stamp Plans Get New Life From Movement of Goods," *Premium Practice* (March, 1967), p. 61.

15. *Look* National Appliance Survey, pp. 15, 31, 107, 113.

16. "Marketing Develops into Alliance for Profit," *Grey Matter,* Vol. 36, No. 6 (New York: Grey Advertising, Inc., 1965).

17. James L. Palmer, "You as a Merchant" (in: *Listen to Leaders in Business* ed. A. Love and J. S. Childers. New York: Holt, Rinehart and Winston, Inc., 1962), p. 85.

18. "The True Look of the Discount Industry, 1964." A special research report by *DM, The Discount Merchandiser.*

19. "Operating Results of Department and Specialty Stores in 1963" (New York: Controllers' Congress, National Retail Merchants Association, 1964), pp. 20 and 69. Used by permission.

20. William R. Davidson and Alton F. Doody, *Retailing Management* (3rd ed. New York: The Ronald Press, 1966), p. 20.

21. Robert G. Drew-Bear, *Self-Service Discount Department Stores,* A Pilot

Research Study (Amhurst, Mass.: University of Massachusetts, Department of Marketing, School of Business Administration, April, 1965), p. 8.

22. "Operating Results of Department and Specialty Stores in 1963," *op. cit.* Note 19 *supra,* p. 4.

23. "Departmental Merchandising and Operating Results of 1964" (New York: Controllers' Congress, National Retail Merchants Association, 1965), p. 3. Used by permission.

24. "How Catalogs Get Their Sales Appeal," *Business Week* (July 25, 1964), p. 98.

25. Report of the Joint Legislative Committee on Commerce and Economic Development, State of New York, Legislative Document No. 84, (1963), p. 1.

26. Milton P. Brown, Wilbur B. England, John B. Matthews, Jr., *Problems in Marketing,* 3rd ed. (New York: McGraw-Hill Book Co., Inc., 1961), pp. 684 and 455.

27. *Ibid.,* p. 685.

28. National Commission on Food Marketing, *Organization and Competition in Food Retailing, op. cit.* in Chapter 3, p. 443.

29. *Moody's Industrial Manual, 1965* (New York: Moody's Investors Service, Inc., 1965), p. 2176.

30. The Sperry and Hutchinson Company, "Annual Report to Stockholders/ For Year Ending December 31, 1966," p. 22.

31. "Operating Results of Department and Specialty Stores in 1963," *op. cit.* Note 19 *supra,* pp. 4, 6. "The summation of typical figures to subtotals and totals [in Table 13] and also the normally accepted mathematical relationship [in the data here referenced] do not always exist [because] many of the independently selected ratios are comprised of samples differing in number and composition of stores due to differences in method of accounting and reporting of information by the companies involved." *Ibid.,* p. 90.

CHAPTER IX

1. C. S. Duncan, "The Economics and Legality of Premium Giving," Journal of Political Economy, Vol. 24 (December, 1924), pp. 921-950.

2. Rast v. Van Deman and Lewis Company, 240 U.S. 365.

3. United States Department of Agriculture, "Trading Stamps and the Consumer's Food Bill" (Washington, D. C.: U. S. Government Printing Office, 1957), p. 5.

4. *Ibid.,* p. 5.

5. Brian J. Strum, *op. cit.* in Chapter 1, p. 1096.

6. *Ibid.*   7. *Ibid.*

8. "Why Don't They Just Cut the Price?" *Changing Times: The Kiplinger Magazine* (April, 1962), p. 11.

9. James D. Bromley and William H. Wallace, *The Effect of Trading Stamps on Retail Food Prices.* Contribution No. 1091 of the Rhode Island Agricultural Experimental Station, Kingston, R. I. (reprint). Reported in June 1964 issue of *Rhode Island Agriculture.*

10. *Ibid.,* p. 8.

11. Letter from Prof. William H. Wallace to the author (July 8, 1966).

12. Letter from Prof. William H. Wallace to the author (Sept. 12, 1966).

13. Weldon J. Taylor and Associates, *Supplement to an Analysis of Trading Stamps in Utah* (Provo, Utah: Brigham Young University, College of Business, n. d.), p. 9.

14. Verne A. Bunn, "Trading Stamps and Retail Food Prices, 1960-1965," Prepared at the request of The Sperry and Hutchinson Company (Kansas City, Mo.: Midwest Research Institute), p. 2.

15. Harvey L. Vredenburg and H. Howard Frisinger, "The Value of Trading Stamps as Measured by Retail Prices," *Journal of Retailing*, New York University, Institute of Retail Management (Fall, 1965), p. 29.

16. *Ibid.*, p. 32.

CHAPTER X

1. Sam Flanel, *Operating Results of Department and Specialty Stores in 1963* (New York: Controllers' Congress, National Retail Merchants Association, 1964), p. 4. Used by permission.

2. Robert G. Drew-Bear, *Merchandising Operations of Self-Service Discount Department Stores: 1963* (Amherst, Mass.: School of Business Administration, University of Massachusetts, 1965), p. 8.

CHAPTER XI

1. United States Department of Agriculture, "Trading Stamps and Their Impact on Food Prices," *op. cit.* in Chapter 1, p. 1.

2. *Ibid.*, p. 20.   3. *Ibid.*, p. iv.

4. "What's Going On In Trading Stamps?" *Progressive Grocer, op. cit.* in Chapter 4, p. 55.

5. Verne A. Bunn, *op. cit.* in Chapter 9, p. 2.

6. *Ibid.*, p. 28.

7. United States Department of Agriculture, "Trading Stamps and Their Impact on Food Prices," *op. cit.* in Chapter 1, p. 19.

8. James D. Bromley and William H. Wallace, *op. cit.* in Chapter 9, p. 4.

9. *Ibid.*, p. 8.

10. Milton Alexander, "An Analysis of a Rhode Island University Study of Trading Stamps and Prices." Report prepared by M. Alexander, Associate Professor of Marketing, Fordham University School of Business, at the request of The Sperry and Hutchinson Company (1965), p. 1.

11. *Ibid.*, p. 4.

12. The Honorable Persia Campbell, Consumer Counsel to the Governor of New York, State Conference on Store Trading Stamps, (October 2, 1956). (Transcript.)

13. R. F. Harrod, "Theory of Imperfect Competition Revised," *Economic Essays*, Essay 8 (New York: Harcourt Brace and Company, Inc., 1952), pp. 153 ff.

14. U. S. Department of Agriculture, "Trading Stamps and Their Impact on Food Prices, *op. cit.* in Chapter 1, p. 22.

15. Robert H. Strotz, "On Being Fooled by Figures: The Case of Trading Stamps," *Journal of Business* (October, 1958), p. 306.

16. "Ad Specials Are No Clue to Retail Prices, Food Marketing Group Finds," *Advertising Age* (July 18, 1966), p. 1.

17. Otto A. Davis, *op. cit.* in Chapter 2, and Ralph L. Andreano, "Effects of Trading Stamps on Retail Competition," *Journal of Retailing* (Summer, 1959), pp. 87-99.

18. Joseph A. Schumpeter, *History of Economic Analysis* (London, England: George Allen and Unwin, Ltd., 1954), p. 241.

19. Sumner H. Slichter, *op. cit.* in Chapter 3, pp. 20-21.

20. W. Arthur Lewis, *Overhead Costs* (London, England: Allen and Unwin, Ltd., 1949), p. 149.

INDEX